WESTERN TIMES

BR (W)

Contents

The Transport Treasury

Front Cover: The BR influence on the (Great) Western Region. '9F' No 92220 Evening Star at the head of the down 'Capitals United Express' prior to leaving Paddington. The year is 1960 and this locomotive is known to have been rostered for this working on 27, 28 June and 1 July; the last named the date of our image. It also worked the 7.43 am Cardiff-Paddington on 18 June. This class evolved into a genuine mixed traffic type and often worked "extras" on summer Saturdays in the west. Some 9Fs, despite their 5' 0" diameter driving wheels, were recorded at speeds up to 90 mph which confounded the traditional belief that 6' plus was essential for express timings, and which underlined the all-round excellence of this design. Once "Authority" learned of what was going on, this practice was promptly prohibited and with good reason. The combination of excessive speed, small driving wheels, substantial reciprocating mass and two cylinders would have generated a high degree of hammer blow. This was bad news for the track, and in the long run for the locomotive. Of course, the "long run" was to be shamefully denied these splendid machines. Douglas Twibell / The Transport Treasury.

Frontispiece: Away from prestigious named trains, it was freight traffic (especially coal) that was the main revenue source for the Western over decades. Here 2-8-2T No 7224 has charge of a mixed freight passing Cardiff Central. (The head code describes a "Through freight or ballast train not working under C, D, E, or F conditions"; such a working was signalled using the bell code '1-4'). The patch-painted first wagon is an ex-private owner vehicle as indicated by the "P" prefix to the number. The photograph is undated but this view is thought to be around about 1960 as the "72" has acquired the BR ferret-and-dartboard totem. The ex-PO wagon would have been of pre-1939 vintage and this category of vehicle was still to be seen at work in reducing numbers in the early 1960s. Ron Roberts

Rear cover: Western Region tubular post stop and distant signals – notice how if there is a distant on the same post, the priority is of course the stop signal hence the finial is painted red. Pressed metal arms bent over on the top and bottom edges for strength and the end of the distant arm does not go to such a sharp point as with the wooden variant. The heavy cast spectacle plate would probably return the arm to 'on' of its own volition should a wire break but the (G)WR took no chances and lower down the post was a balance weight for each. In *Western Times* we want to get things right so we do welcome comments and additional information. Sadly just because it may appear in print or on a website does not always mean it is fact, as witness one book on WR signalling of recent years where it was stated by no less a man than a member of a professional institute that a signalman could never restore the stop arm to danger until the train had cleared all the track circuits ahead... .

© Images and design: The Transport Treasury 2021.

ISBN 978-1-913251-19-2

First Published in 2021 by Transport Treasury Publishing Ltd.,
16 Highworth Close, High Wycombe, HP13 7PJ

www.ttpublishing.co.uk   *or for editorial issues and contributions email to*   WesternTimes@mail.com

Printed in the UK by Henry Ling Limited at the Dorset Press. Dorchester DT1 1HD

Copies of many of the images within WESTERN TIMES are available for purchase/download.
In addition the Transport Treasury Archive contains tens of thousands of other UK,
Irish and some European railway photographs.

INTRODUCTION

Welcome to the inaugural issue of *Western Times*, a half yearly periodical devoted to exploring and reporting on all aspects of the Great Western Railway, and its continuation as the "Great Western Region" of British Railways.

The GWR has been described and recorded countless times in print and on film making it arguably the most thoroughly documented of any of the world's transport undertakings. Further, a well-known dealer in scrap metal had the wisdom first to locate his business firmly in GWR territory and then to take a key decision over stock control that allowed many precious items to make a further journey, away from the cutting torch and into the capable hands of the preservation movement. These acts of rescue were the catalyst for conservation of so much more in the way of mobile assets, infrastructure, ephemera, minutiae and even lines of route.

Today, among the Big Four, the GWR today enjoys the greatest physical representation. Devotees of the Old Company can truly rejoice in the survival of so much more than could ever have been dreamed possible in the grim early 1960s. Then the railway network appeared to be in serious, possibly terminal, decline epitomised by battered, filthy, anonymous Halls that fostered the sense of impending and complete loss.

The near miraculous recovery of the last half century at the hands of the dedicated volunteer army suggests that the "Great Western market" might have become saturated, and that no room remains for a specialist publication. Extended debate over several months has drawn a contrary conclusion to the extent that Transport Treasury Publishing in conjunction with the editorial team is prepared to commit money, time, research and plenty of hard work in the establishment of *Western Times*, and in ensuring its success.

The GWR as it stands today flourishes on the commitment of the preservation movement and on the support of the railway press at commercial and society level. Inevitably this is principally through the prism of what exists today. These efforts are vital but they do risk diminishing attention on what went before, and with the passing of the generations, much that is held in the collective memories of devotees will be lost. The parallel with the early 1960s is obvious. Then, fear was based on irredeemable disappearance of treasured artefacts. Today, that fear has resurfaced through the concern that memories, records, photographs, reminiscences also deserve preservation before it is too late.

In planning *Western Times*, decisions were taken about the publication's parameters and it is important to share these with the readership:-

Beginning – the GWR celebrated its Centenary in 1935 so the historic scope goes to 1835.

Ending – withdrawal of the last diesel-hydraulic Class D1000 from ordinary service marked termination of Western individualism (and idiosyncrasy) in motive power matters. Accordingly for *Western Times*, the story ends in 1977.

Exclusions – the GWR preservation movement started to gather momentum around about 1960. Thus matters arising in the following seventeen years will concern only the ordinary service railway, and any contributions whose primary focus is the preservation scene will not be accepted. This policy does not preclude occasional reference to saved artefacts and assets where historic comparison is appropriate, but there is no overt intention to trespass into a field so well supported by other publications.

Accuracy – in creating and developing a historical record, accuracy is paramount but cannot be guaranteed through the efforts of contributors and the editorial team alone. A working co-operation with the readership is invited and correspondence that amplifies, corrects or contradicts is welcome. Published acknowledgement will be given with the intention of stimulating further debate and of extracting previously undisclosed but valuable information.

Impartiality – the Old Company was a large and complex business. Any pretence that it was as near perfect as many have sought to assert is a great disservice to its memory. The image sustained by glittering Castles, Centenary stock, Dawlish sea wall, the Paddington-Bristol race track etc is a minuscule representation of the whole. This selectivity does little to measure the *texture* of an organisation that embraced much that was admirable but also much that was unimpressive. Too many writers have wilfully chosen to ignore the negatives, preferring their views to be swayed by sentiment. This re-writing detracts from the objective and informative recording of an organisation dear to so many.

Accordingly, a mission summary for 'Western Times' could well be.........the Great Western Railway: the everyday reality.

--- o O o---

Editors: Andrew Malthouse and Kevin Robertson

Editorial assistant: Jeremy Clements

GREAT WESTERN RAILWAY

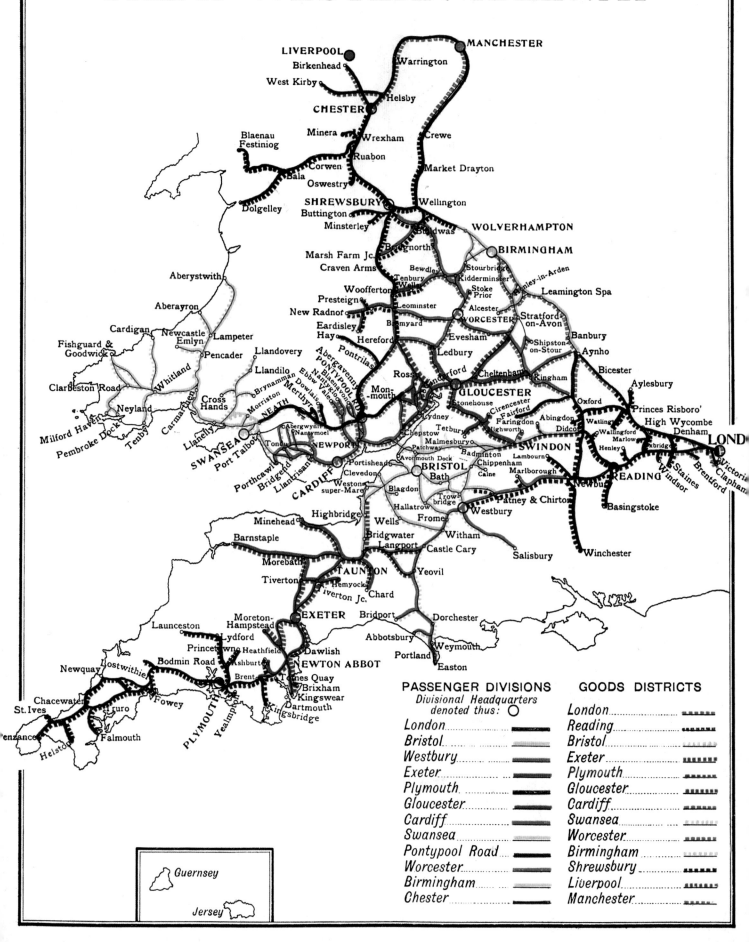

PASSENGER DIVISIONS	GOODS DISTRICTS
Divisional Headquarters denoted thus: ◯	
London	London
Bristol	Reading
Westbury	Bristol
Exeter	Exeter
Plymouth	Plymouth
Gloucester	Gloucester
Cardiff	Cardiff
Swansea	Swansea
Pontypool Road	Worcester
Worcester	Birmingham
Birmingham	Shrewsbury
Chester	Liverpool
	Manchester

Guernsey

Jersey

THE GWR TRAFFIC, LOCOMOTIVE AND ENGINEERING DIVISIONS

By route mileage, the GWR was the largest of the pre-Grouping companies making it necessary to administer the organisation through a divisional structure that recognised both geographic and technical areas of responsibility. The extent and diversity of these divisions was defined in a series of diagrammatic maps issued by Paddington. In this and succeeding issues, these maps will be illustrated together with background comments to explain the complexity of the company's organisation. The first appears opposite and shows segmentation of the network in respect of the two main income sources – goods and passenger traffic. Divisional responsibility was easily defined at some locations such as Exeter which was the focal point of the relative Passenger and Goods divisions. In contrast the situation was more complex at Aynho where London, Birmingham & Worcester Passenger, and Worcester Goods divisions converged.

This map appeared in the *Railway Gazette* of 5 November 1915 and was taken from a pamphlet entitled *Organisation of the Passenger, Goods, Locomotive, Engineering etc Departments* issued by Frank Potter, General Manager. He appears to have recognised the negative aspects of the divisional/ district structure through the following statement:

The ideal organisation is that which accomplished the object for which it is called into being with the minimum of power, noise, fuss and friction, and the maximum of efficiency. It secures the best men for each class of work and for each particular duty and looks ahead to provide for the replacing of those men by training others to take their place in due course. A big organisation must have its departments and sections, but it is only insofar as they are not only integral and indispensable parts of the whole, but as all are co-related that each part assists and further the object of others. Each individual member of a department must remember that his department is only self-contained to secure the due development of its functions to the whole organisation.

The pamphlet's title placed "Passenger" first presumably acknowledging the company's operational shop window whereas with "Goods" was by far the greater revenue source then and for the remainder of the company's existence. "Locomotive", the prime focus of most enthusiastic interest came third. "Engineering etc" was a catch-all that embraced numerous divergent activities. Potter's key point was that each divisional/ district activity could only be truly effective through efficient inter-action with others.

The GWR (in modern management-speak) was vertically integrated in manufacturing most of the fixed and mobile assets that it operated. There were a few notable exceptions - for example steel rails, breakdown cranes by Ransomes & Rapier, and that rarest of surviving artefacts, miniature bottles [full] of highly regarded GWR Scotch whisky. The company was thus a major manufacturer in addition to its obligations as a transport company. Perhaps the most profound railway industry change since the 1950s has been the progressive shedding of many functions by out-sourcing them to contractors.

Inset: This is the cover of the Appendix to the Service Time Tables for February 1943. The area covered by No 12 Section in this 1943 edition differs from those of earlier years. Exactly when these books were issued for each division plus how often revisions followed is uncertain. Some examples can be readily traced but others are very rare. We hope to feature the contents of a typical example in a later edition of WT together with details of how many issues for each area were actually provided. Historically, they are an invaluable information source. Details of the Section Number, area and date for any examples in readers' collections and a scan/ photograph of the front cover would be greatly appreciated.

GREAT WESTERN RAILWAY
APPENDIX
to No. 12 SECTION of the
Service Time Tables
WORCESTER, HEREFORD AND NEWPORT

February, 1943
AND UNTIL FURTHER NOTICE

Opposite: Extract from The Railway Gazette 1916. Accompanying the original article was a second coloured drawing showing the Engineering and Locomotive divisions which appears overleaf. More detail describing the exact area of responsibility and actual boundary points was provided in tabular form together with the names of the responsible divisional and senior officers. Some examples are shewn on the following pages but this information has been abridged to save space.

GREAT WESTERN RAILWAY

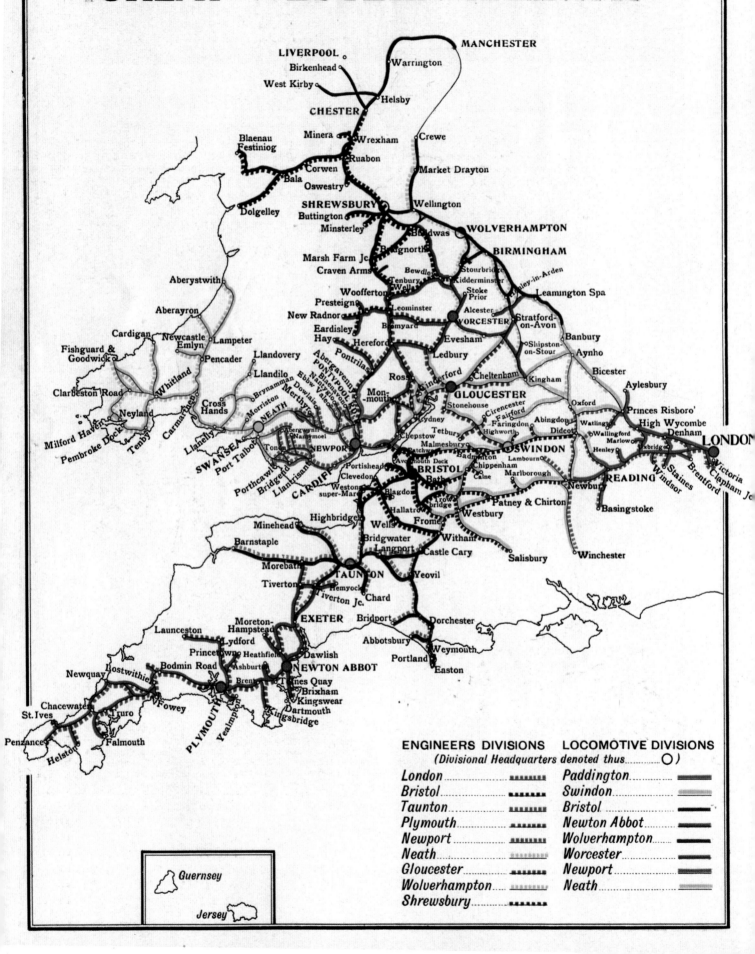

MANCHESTER

LIVERPOOL
Birkenhead
West Kirby
Warrington
Helsby
CHESTER
Minera
Wrexham
Crewe
Blaenau Festiniog
Ruabon
Market Drayton
Corwen
Bala
Oswestry
Wellington
Dolgelley
SHREWSBURY
Buttington
WOLVERHAMPTON
Minsterley
Buildwas
Bridgnorth
BIRMINGHAM
Marsh Farm Jc.
Bewdley
Stourbridge
Craven Arms
Kidderminster
Henley-in-Arden
Aberystwith
Tenbury Wells
Stoke Prior
Leamington Spa
Woofferton
Alcester
Stratford-on-Avon
Aberayron
Presteign
Leominster
WORCESTER
Cardigan
New Radnor
Bromyard
Shipston-on-Stour
Banbury
Newcastle Emlyn
Lampeter
Eardisley
Hay
Hereford
Evesham
Aynho
Fishguard & Goodwick
Pencader
Ledbury
Bicester
Llandovery
Abergavenny
Ross
Ledbury
Cheltenham
Aylesbury
Whitland
Llandilo
PONTYPOOL
Monmouth
Mitcheldean
Kingham
Clarbeston Road
N. Blaenavon
GLOUCESTER
Oxford
Princes Risboro'
Neyland
Carmarthen
Cross Hands
Brynamman
Merthyr
Ebbw Vale
Stonehouse
Cirencester
High Wycombe
Denham
Milford Haven
Morriston
NEATH
Dowlais
Cydney
Tetbury
Fairford
Faringdon
Abingdon
Watlington
Wallingford
Marlow
LONDON
Pembroke Dock
Tenby
Llanelly
Abergwynfi
Nantymoel
Tondu
NEWPORT
Chepstow
Malmesbury
Highworth
Didcot
Henley
Uxbridge
Victoria
Clapham Jc.
SWANSEA
Port Talbot
Porthcawl
Bridgend
Llantrisant
CARDIFF
Portishead
Clevedon
Weston-super-Mare
Patchway
Avonmouth Dock
BRISTOL
Bath
SWINDON
Chippenham
Calne
Lambourn
Marlborough
Newbury
READING
Windsor
Staines
Brentford
Basingstoke
Blagdon
Trowbridge
Westbury
Patney & Chirton
Highbridge
Wells
Frome
Winchester
Minehead
Bridgwater
Langport
Hallatrow
Witham
Barnstaple
Castle Cary
Salisbury
Morebath
TAUNTON
Yeovil
Tiverton
Hemyock
Chard
Tiverton Jc.
EXETER
Bridport
Dorchester
Launceston
Moreton-Hampstead
Lydford
Princetown
Heathfield
Dawlish
Abbotsbury
Weymouth
Bodmin Road
Ashburton
Portland
Easton
Newquay
Lostwithiel
Brent
NEWTON ABBOT
Totnes Quay
Brixham
Fowey
Kingswear
Dartmouth
Chacewater
Truro
PLYMOUTH
Yealmpton
Kingsbridge
St. Ives
Helston
Falmouth
Penzance

ENGINEERS DIVISIONS
(Divisional Headquarters denoted thus .... ◯)

London
Bristol
Taunton
Plymouth
Newport
Neath
Gloucester
Wolverhampton
Shrewsbury

LOCOMOTIVE DIVISIONS

Paddington
Swindon
Bristol
Newton Abbot
Wolverhampton
Worcester
Newport
Neath

Guernsey

Jersey

The Divisional Management Hierarchy in 1915

Passenger Dept. Paddington	Goods Dept. Paddington	Loco & Carriage Dept. Swindon	Engineering Dept. Paddington	Signal Dept. Reading
C Aldington *Superintendant of the Line*	**C A Roberts** *Chief Goods Manager*	**F G Wright** *Assistant Superintendant*	**W W Grierson** *Engineer*	**A T Blackall** *Signal Engineer*
R H Nichols *Assistant to the Superintendant of the Line*	**J P Monkhouse** *Assistant to Chief Goods Manager*	**H C King** *Assistant to the Superintendant*	**W Y Armstrong** *New Works Engineer*	**R J Insell** *Chief Assistant*
F C A Coventry *Assistant to the Superintendant of the Line*	**F B Mortimer** *Assistant Goods Manager (Rates Dept.)*	**C B Collett** *Locomotive Works Manager*		**C M Jacobs** *Electrical Assistant*
S A Pope *Assistant to the Superintendant of the Line*	**W J S Cox** *Assistant Goods Manager (Coal Dept.)*	**F W Marillier** *Carriage and Wagon Works Manager*	**Outdoor Superintendants**	
C Gibbs *Telegraph Assistant to Superintendant of the Line*	**F W Barber** *Assistant to Chief Goods Manager (Representative and Live Stock Dept.)*		**W H Williams** *Swindon* **J A Robinson** *Wolverhampton*	

Areas of different departmental responsibilities are evident in this recently discovered image, with the exception of the Passenger Department. Date and location are unknown (can any reader help?) but several features require comment.

The reason for the double balance weight at the foot of the starting signal is not certain. It might have been dictated by a convoluted route for the wire from the box and the need to overcome greater frictional resistance on returning to "On" – an example of the GWR's commitment to safety. Alternatively but less likely, the arm was slotted with another box. Note also the warning bell attached to the post.

The railway was an major medium for advertising income and expense. Mounted on the fencing to the left are three enamelled tin signs. If it related to a local brewery that for "???EAD'S Stout & Ale" might provide a clue regarding location. The other two are for Pear's Soap and Dewar's Whisky – both ubiquitous around the network. The painted advert on the brickwork of the building end to the right states GREAT WESTERN RAILWAY COMPANY. GENERAL CARRIERS TO ALL PARTS OF ENGLAND WALES SCOTLAND IRELAND AND THE CHANNEL ISLANDS. Unless the building was company-owned, this would have been an expense.

The train is of the Edwardian era and reference to the company's *Engine Head Signals* for 1905 indicates that this was an Express Cattle or Goods Train, Class B. The load includes general merchandise in sheeted wagons and coal in 7-plank private owner wagons. The motive power is Class 388 Standard Goods No. 789 (built October 1873, withdrawn December 1921) and is fitted with a Type S4 boiler (carried by this locomotive January 1900 to July 1905 and May 1908 to January 1915). More information about this class appears on pages 50 to 56.

GEOGRAPHICAL AREAS OF DEPARTMENTAL RESPONSIBILITY WITHIN EACH DISTRICT			
Passenger Divisions	**Goods Districts**	**Locomotive Divisions**	**Engineering Divisions**
1 London	**1 London**	**1 Paddington**	**1 Paddington**
Main line to Didcot, Foxhall Junction (inclusive) and branches. *Reading to Enborne Junction (inclusive) and branches.* *London to Aynho Junction (inclusive) and branches.* *Didcot to Aynho Junction (inclusive) and branches (exclusive) of the Kingham branch.*	*London Stations, Depots and Docks (including Tilbury Docks).* *Main line to Hayes (inclusive) and branch to Brentford.* *Wycombe District Line from Old Oak Common to Northolt Junction (exclusive).*	*Paddington to Pangbourne.* *Reading to Newbury Racecourse (exclusive).* *Old Oak Common West to Princes Risborough.* *All branches from sections shown above.*	*Main line from Paddington to Steventon (exclusive) 56¼ m.p. and branches.* *Paddington to Princes Risborough (except High Wycombe (exclusive) to Ashendon Junction and Aylesbury), and Kennington Junction and branches.* *Reading to Newbury (inclusive) 54m 21ch.* *Didcot to Winchester.* *Didcot to Kennington Junction (inclusive) 61¼ m.p.*

Churchward Mogul (perhaps No. 4360) at the east end of Salisbury LSWR station with what is a through goods from the GWR to the Southern. Between London and Exeter there were six such interchange points for traffic between the two companies; the west London line, Basingstoke, Andover, Salisbury, Yeovil and of course Exeter itself. GWR engines would come off at Salisbury and be replaced by Southern motive power following which the usual destination would be Eastleigh for remarshalling. In the right background is the former GWR terminus which boasted two platform lines plus two centre sidings.

2 Bristol	2 Reading	2 Swindon	2 Bristol
Main line from Didcot, Foxhall Junction (exclusive) to Durston Junction (exclusive) and branches other than Gloucester. Wootton Bassett to South Wales end of Severn Tunnel and branches. Thingley Junction to Westbury (exclusive) and branches.	Main line, West Drayton to Didcot and branches. GW & GC Joint from Northolt Junction to Haddenham and branches to Aylesbury and Uxbridge High Street. Didcot to Oxford, inclusive of Wolvercote Siding, and branches to Abingdon, Bledlow and Watlington. Didcot, Newbury and Southampton Junction line. Reading to Seend (including Basingstoke and other branches) and Stert and Westbury line (exclusive of Westbury). Kennet and Avon Canal between Reading and Seend.	Pangbourne (exclusive) to Box. Wootton Bassett to Chipping Sodbury. Thingley Junction to Westbury. Newbury Racecourse to Witham (exclusive). Patney & Chirton via Holt Junction to Bathampton (exclusive). Frome to Radstock (exclusive). Didcot to Fenny Compton. Kennington Junction to Princes Risborough (exclusive). Aynho via Bicester to Princes Risborough (exclusive). Wolvercote Junction to Kingham. King's Sutton to Cheltenham. Swindon to Woolaston. Cheltenham to Honeybourne (exclusive). Gloucester to Ledbury (exclusive). Grange Court to Ross (exclusive). Severn and Wye Railway. All branches from sections shown above.	Main line from Steventon (inclusive) 56¼ m.p. to Brent Knoll (inclusive) 149m 49ch, and branches. South Wales and Bristol Direct Railway and branch. Newbury (exclusive) 54m 21ch to Holt Junction and branches. Patney and Chirton to Westbury, and Salisbury branch. Thingley Junction to Witham (inclusive) 121 m.p. and branches. Bristol and South Wales end of Severn Tunnel, except Ashley Hill Junction to Avonmouth and Hotwells (GW & Midland Joint Lines).

Snakes alive – and nothing to do with the famous notice on the Princetown branch. A pet grass snake carried in a box by a boy travelling from Birmingham to Stourbridge escaped when the box lid was opened and disappeared into the upholstery. After a search at Stourbridge Junction the train went on with the compartment locked, in case the snake should escape and alarm passengers. The coach was subsequently stripped of upholstery at Cardiff but it was still not found. A final recourse was for the vehicle to be taken to Swindon where it was put into the disinfectant chamber and after treatment 'Hissing Sid' was no more. From the *Railway Magazine*, July 1958.

3 Westbury	3 Bristol	3 Bristol	3 Taunton
Enborne Junction (exclusive) to Athelney; the Marlborough and Salisbury branches; Castle Cary to Easton and branches.	*Swindon (exclusive) via Chippenham to Bleadon and Uphill (exclusive) and branches.* *Wootton Bassett to Pilning and branches.* *Chippenham to Salisbury and Weymouth but exclusive of lines Castle Cary and Yeovil to Langport.* *Kennet and Avon Canal between Seend (exclusive) and Hanham Mills.*	*Box (exclusive) to Tiverton Junction (exclusive).* *Bristol to Pilning.* *Filton to Chipping Sodbury (exclusive).* *Bristol to Radstock.* *Hallatrow to Limpley Stoke (exclusive).* *Yatton to Witham.* *Witham to Cogload Junction.* *Castle Cary to Weymouth.* *All branches from sections shown above.*	*Main line from Brent Knoll (exclusive) 143m 49ch to Exeter St Davids (inclusive) 194m 10ch and branches.* *Witham (exclusive) 121 m.p. to Weymouth and branches.* *Castle Cary 115m 38ch to Cogload Junction 137m 69ch.* *Bridgwater and Taunton and Great Western Canals and River Tone Navigation.*

Opposite page: From 1932 all passenger traffic was concentrated on the LSWR station at Salisbury with the former GWR facilities used for stock storage. From photographs, it is evident that a wide variety of motive made its way down from Westbury, with the exception of the 'King' and '47xx' classes, but the presence of work-stained 2-8-0T No 4228 raises questions.

These engines were late additions to Churchward's design and construction programme. They were specifically intended for heavier Welsh coal trains over comparatively short distances for which their unusual wheel arrangement made them ideally suited. Excellent performers, their range of operations was limited by lack of rear end space and thus a 3-ton coal capacity. Apart from the St. Blazey contingent of two, sometimes three, over many years to work china clay trains, allocations to English depots were quite unusual. During a career lasting from November 1913 to December 1963, No. 4228 was a wanderer being allocated to nine Welsh sheds, in three cases more than once, plus Bristol (presumably SPAM) during October/ November 1917 and Old Oak Common from December 1930 until June 1932. None of this explains its presence at Salisbury; perhaps it was substituting for failed 2-8-2T Class 72xx which was the favoured motive power on South Wales-Salisbury coal trains.

The freshly painted brake van No. 5688? is a Toad Diagram AA2, 278 examples of which were built between 1902 and 1910.

4 Exeter	4 Exeter	4 Newton Abbot	4 Plymouth
Main line from Durston Junction (exclusive) to Brent (exclusive) and branches, other than that from Durston.	*Bleadon and Uphill to Ashburton Junction (exclusive) and branches including lines to Castle Cary and Yeovil (both exclusive).* *Bridgwater Dock and Dock Lines, Grand Western Canal, Bridgwater and Taunton, and River Tone Navigation Canals.*	*Tiverton Junction to Penzance.* *Stoke Canon to Morebath Junction (exclusive).* *All branches from sections shown above.*	*Main line from Exeter St Davids (exclusive) 194m 10ch to Penzance and branches.* *Stover Canal.*

5 Plymouth	5 Plymouth	5 Wolverhampton	5 Newport
Main line from Brent (inclusive) to Penzance and branches.	*Ashburton Junction to Penzance and branches.*	*Fenny Compton (exclusive) to Birkenhead.* *Wellington to Crewe.* *Chester to Manchester.* *Tyseley to Bearley (exclusive).* *Handsworth Junction to Stourbridge Junction.* *Priestfield to Kidderminster (exclusive).* *Shrewsbury to Ludlow.* *Sutton Bridge Junction to Buildwas.* *Marsh Farm Junction to Madeley Junction.* *All branches from sections shown above.*	*South Wales main line from Chepstow (exclusive) 142m 35ch to Pyle (inclusive) 196½ m.p. and branches.* *Newport to Little Mill Junction (exclusive).* *Pontypool Road to Hirwain (inclusive) 26½ m.p. except GW & Rhymney Joint Lines.* *Rhondda & Swansea Bay Railway, Treherbert to Pontrhydyfen, 10 m.p.*

Some years ago a collection of 150+ glass negatives was loaned to one of your editors and known as the Shaftsbury collection. The name taken from the town where this box of priceless material was found in a second hand shop. Fortunately there was an index of sorts whilst even better, perusal revealed most to be of GW subjects around the 1930s. Many were recorded in the Salisbury area, static views rather than moving images but explained by the slow film of the period. We do not believe any have been seen before and we are delighted to present a small selection with more to follow in future issues of *Western Times*.

6 Gloucester	6 Gloucester	6 Worcester	6 Neath
Swindon (exclusive) to Wye Valley Junction (exclusive) and branches.	Didcot (exclusive) to Swindon and Gloucester, and branches.	Kingham (exclusive) to Kidderminster.	South Wales main line from Pyle (exclusive) 196½ m.p. to Neyland, and Fishguard Harbour and branches.
Gloucester to Ledbury (exclusive).	Gloucester to Ledbury (exclusive), Hereford, Monmouth (exclusive), Woolaston and branches.	Honeybourne to Hatton (exclusive).	Hirwain (exclusive) 26½ m.p. to Swansea and Neath Loop.
Grange Court to Holme Lacey.		Worcester to Hereford.	
Gloucester to Kingham (exclusive) and Honeybourne (exclusive).	Cheltenham to Kingham (exclusive) and Honeybourne (exclusive).	Ludlow (exclusive) to Llanvihangel (exclusive).	Rhondda & Swansea Bay Railway, Pontrhydyfen 10 m.p. to Swansea and branches.
Hereford Barton and Kington branches.		Hereford to Monmouth May Hill (exclusive).	
Ross to Monmouth (exclusive).		Hartlebury Junction to Buildwas (exclusive).	
Forest of Dean and Coleford branches.		Kidderminster to Woofferton.	
Great Western working interests on the L&NW and GW Joint Lines on section: Redhill Junction to Woofferton and Tenbury Wells.		All branches from sections shown above.	

Opposite: The Bulldog "4-4-0"s were attractive, workmanlike medium-sized engines whose complex early history is reflected in the development of No. 3300. This locomotive started life in May 1895 as No. 3253, the second member of the "Duke of Cornwall" or more commonly the "Duke" Class. In November 1908, it was withdrawn for rebuilding as a Bulldog. This process entailed replacement of the original parallel type S4 boiler with a Standard No. 2 that was heavier with a larger heating surface (twenty Dukes were so treated between 1902 and 1909). Further changes followed with installation of superheating in November 1911 and piston valves in February 1918. It later acquired Automatic Train Control as can be seen in this photograph, and withdrawal came in January 1936. The names carried by the Dukes and the Bulldogs were an eclectic collection, in contrast to the later preference for the private addresses of the nobility and gentry. In the late 1920s and early 1930s, a number of Bulldogs named after towns and cities were reduced to numbers only on the grounds that passengers might mistake a locomotive's nameplate for the destination of its train. *Penzance* (No. 3377) and *Paddington* (No 3386) were targets of this policy although *Vancouver* (No. 3401) and *Bombay* (No. 3408) were considered safe. No 3300 was an early casualty of the de-naming process as in May 1923 its name, *Pendennis Castle*, was needed elsewhere. The train, either a horse box special or a local working having at least three 'Pacos' at its head is awaiting departure from Salisbury.

7 Cardiff	7 Cardiff	7 Newport	7 Gloucester
Wye Valley Junction and South Wales end of Severn Tunnel to Pyle and branches.	Woolaston (exclusive) to Pencoed (exclusive) and branches.	Woolaston (exclusive) to Pyle.	South Wales main line from Swindon (exclusive) 77½ m.p. to Chepstow (inclusive) 142m 35ch and branches.
Newport to Panteg Junction.	Monmouth and Hirwain and branches.	Little Mill Junction to Monmouth May Hill.	
Newport (Dock Street).	Newport to Hereford (exclusive) and Golden Valley line.	Pontypool Road to Hirwain Pond.	Honeybourne and Cheltenham line from ½ m.p. to Cheltenham.
Wye Valley line (excluding Monmouth).		Severn Tunnel Junction to Pilning (exclusive).	Cheltenham to Stow-on-the-Wold (inclusive).
Eastern and Western (Monmouthshire) Valleys.	Monmouthshire & Brecon and Abergavenny Canals.	Newport to Llanvihangel.	Leominster (inclusive) and Worcester Foregate Street (inclusive) to Little Mill Junction (inclusive) and branches, except Tramway Junction (Gloucester) to Churchdown (exclusive), also Severn and Wye Joint Lines north of Parkend.
Penar Branch.		All branches from sections shown above.	
Ely Valley and Llynvi and Ogmore branches.			

8 Swansea	8 Swansea	8 Neath	8 Wolverhampton
Pyle to Fishguard and Neyland branches.	*Stations west of Llanharen, Pencoed (but including Pencoed), Hendreforgan and Hirwain.*	*Pyle (exclusive) to Fishguard Harbour.* *Swansea (Vale of Neath) to Hirwain Pond (exclusive).* *Rhondda & Swansea Bay Railway.* *All branches from sections shown above.*	*Kennington Junction (exclusive) 61½ m.p. to Wellington (exclusive) and branches.* *Wolvercote Junction to Worcester and Wolverhampton and branches north of line.* *Stourbridge Extension Canal.* *Market Drayton branch.*
9 Pontypool Road	**9 Worcester**	**9 Port Talbot**	**9 Shrewsbury**
Redhill Junction, Hereford (exclusive) to Pontypool Road and Neath Junction (exclusive) via Aberdare and branches.	*Wolvercote Junction to Stourbridge Junction (exclusive).* *Coalport (exclusive) and branches, including those to Tenbury Wells, Leominster and Hereford (all exclusive).* *Wolvercote and Ashendon Junctions to Tyseley Junction (via Earleswood Lakes and Solihull) and branches, including the Fairford branch, but excluding the Cheltenham to Kingham and Cheltenham to Honeybourne branches.* *Stratford-on-Avon Canal.*	*Port Talbot Railway.*	*Shrewsbury to Saltney Junction and branches.* *Shrewsbury to Leominster (exclusive) and Kidderminster (exclusive) and Hartlebury Junction (exclusive) and branches west of the latter.* *Buildwas to Lightmoor Junction (exclusive).*

10 Worcester	10 Birmingham		10 Port Talbot Railways
Yarnton Junction (exclusive) to Stourbridge Junction (exclusive). Worcester to Hereford (exclusive) and the following branches: Worcester, Bromyard, Leominster (Leominster exclusive). King's Sutton (exclusive) to Kingham. Stoke Works. Severn Valley (Burnt Mill Junction exclusive). Tenbury Wells (exclusive) to Kidderminster. Buildwas and Craven Arms (to Marsh Farm Junction exclusive). Moreton-in-Marsh and Shipston-on-Stour Tramway.	Tyseley Junction to Oxley Sidings, thence to Stourbridge Junction, including all branches. Stourbridge Extension Canal.		Port Talbot Company's line.

Opposite: Shunting duty for 57xx No. 7730 complete with short wheelbase diagram M1, Lot 256 shunters truck No. 41818. A fireman's shovel has been lodged behind the upper hand rail – a popular position for storage of this implement – while the pep pipe and a fire iron have been "parked" alongside the cab. The GWR and LSWR originally had duplicated facilities at Salisbury including motive power depots. In 1934, the GWR's allocation included an 0-6-0PT, a Dean Goods, thee 28xx, three Bulldogs, and two Moguls but by the end of 1947, this had shrunk to just an 0-6-0PT and two Halls. The shed closed completely in November 1950. In the background is Salisbury signal box which opened in May 1900 having 95 levers; it bears a non-standard identity board beneath the chimney which states "SALISBURY GWR SIGNAL BOX". Under British Railways it was renamed 'Salisbury C' in the Southern style and was closed in November 1973.

In the background to the right a sign advertises the presence of Marcroft Wagons Ltd, ??? Sidings, Radstock, Cardiff & Port Talbot. This firm was one of several engaged in provision of construction, repair and hire services to the vast private owner wagon sector.

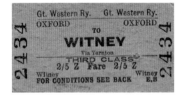

11 Birmingham	11 Shrewsbury		11 Canals Department
Main line to the North from Aynho Junction (exclusive) to Oxley Sidings (inclusive), with branches to Stourbridge Junction, Honeybourne East Junction (exclusive), Alcester and Henley-in-Arden.	Hereford (exclusive) to Shrewsbury, including New Radnor, Eardisley and Presteign branches, and branches to Tenbury Wells, Clee Hill, Buildwas, Minsterley and Buttington. Shrewsbury to Codsall and Coalport branches. Shrewsbury to Balderton (exclusive), Dolgelley, Blaenau Ffestiniog and branches. Wellington to Crewe.		Kennet and Avon Canal. Brecon and Abergavenny Canal. Monmouthshire Canal. Stratford-on-Avon Canal. Swansea Canal. Kennet Navigation. Avon Navigation (Bath to Hanham). Somerset Coal Canal (disused).

12 Chester	12 Liverpool		13 Manchester
Oxley Sidings to Shrewsbury and branches.	*Balderton to Birkenhead, Liverpool, West Kirby and Warrington, and branches.*		*Manchester and the North of England generally.*
Lines North of Shrewsbury.			
Great Western working interests on the L&NW and GW Joint Lines between:		**The numbered headings and likewise the order shown are as per the original *Railway Gazette* article.**	
Woofferton (exclusive) and Shrewsbury with Minsterley and Buttington branches.			
Shrewsbury and Wellington and Coed Talon.			
Chester and Birkenhead and branches.			

Next time we continue with a brief resumé of the Passenger Divisions and Goods Districts shewing responsibility for Great Western interests beyond that already indicated.

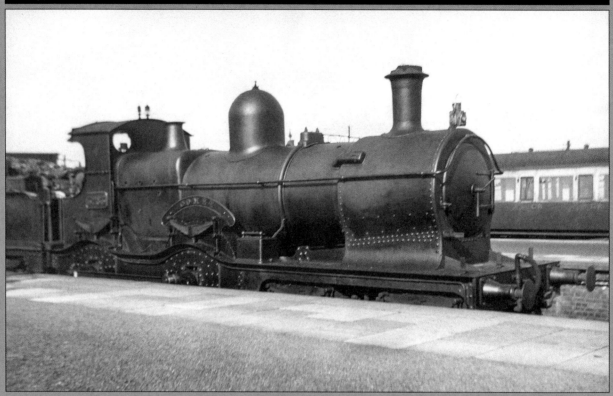

Opposite top: Didcot was home to sundry veteran locomotives from before the war until around 1950. One such resident was Duke Class No 3283 *Comet*, built March 1899 and withdrawn December 1950. Originally numbered 3315, *Comet* was the first of the class to receive a Belpaire firebox (in November 1903) while retaining its original narrow cab. Most of the class later fitted with Belpaire fireboxes concurrently also had wide cabs installed. This photograph was taken at Didcot on 26 February 1939. A lot of nameplate for a short name once proved too tempting for a fiscally conscious wag who scribed in the grime with his finger 'IN' before and 'AX' after.

Opposite bottom: In this view dated circa 1938, Duke Class No 3280 is seen stabled at an unknown location between a Bulldog and a Dean Goods. Built in March 1897, this locomotive was fitted with a Belpaire firebox in October 1913 and concurrently received a wider cab (unlike *Comet*). From new until July 1930, it carried the name *Tregenna* when this was removed to avoid confusion with the 4-6-0 named *Tregenna Castle*.

This page, top: Bulldog No 3366 was at Worcester on 12 March 1939. This locomotive had been built in February 1902 with the name *Earl of Cork*, which was removed in 1936 to avoid confusion with the Earl class 4-4-0s then being introduced, later nicknamed 'Dukedogs'. Unnamed No 3366 worked until April 1948.

This page, right: Bulldog Nos 3320 to 3360 carried unusual oval-shaped combined name and number plates on the cabsides, as in the case of No 3223 *Etona*. The archives contain no supporting detail concerning this locomotive which was officially withdrawn in August 1935. Dick Riley is thought to have taken his first photographs at Swindon in the summer of 1937 so presumably the locomotive had been withdrawn and was awaiting cutting-up but still carrying its identity. *Etona* is the Latin equivalent of Eton.

This page: Bulldog No 3418 *Sir Arthur Yorke* was at Worcester shed on 12 March 1939. Built in June 1906, this locomotive was not named until March 1916, and withdrawn in August 1949. Sir Arthur Yorke was Chief Inspector of Railways (1900-1913) and a director of the GWR (1914-1930). (The chimney is cut off on the negative.)

Opposite top: The fifteen members of the 'Bird' series were the last of the Bulldog class to be introduced. No 3453 *Penguin* (originally No 3742) was built in January 1910 and worked until April 1948. In this view taken on 27th November 1938, *Penguin* minus its tender was awaiting attention at Swindon. The Birds were always distinguishable from the standard, straight running plate Bulldogs in their deeper, stronger outside frames around the driving axles.

Opposite bottom: The short-lived Earl class was introduced in May 1936, by which a Duke boiler was mounted on a Bulldog running chassis. No 3206 *Earl of Plymouth* using frames from Bulldog No 3428 entered service in November 1936. In the June-July 1937. The thirteen engines by then in service lost their Earl names and ran with numbers only (and nicknamed "Dukedogs") until the end of their careers which in the case of No 3206 (later No 9006) was August 1948.

From the *Great Western Magazine*, 1915. "The death is announced of Mr H I Branfield, whose family have for 40 years been the official rat-catchers to the company. On one occasion, Mr Branfield secured over 90 live rats, which he imprisoned in a cage. Coming home in the train he transferred 20 of the rats from the cage to a sack. He then fell asleep, but was aroused by the rats, which had eaten a hole in the sack, running around the compartment, one being actually up his sleeve."

Above: Dukedog No. 3215 had been fitted with top feed in this undated photograph. No details have been recorded in the Archive for this locomotive

Opposite: The last 4-4-0 to be allocated to Didcot was restored City Class No. 3440 *City of Truro*. Here, the celebrity has wandered on to foreign metals and is at Norwood Junction Shed on special duty working in company with ex-LBSCR Mogul No. 32348.

No. 2 in this series will be 'Castles by the Sea'.

TRAFFIC DEPARTMENT. August Bank Holiday Traffic. To provide for the heavy passenger traffic during the August Bank Holiday period it was necessary to duplicate many of the through expresses on several days. On Saturday, July 31, the principal through express trains from and to Paddington, and also the cross-country services, were duplicated, and in some cases triplicated; the holiday traffic to the ever-popular West of England was exceedingly heavy; the 'Cornish Riviera' express had to be run in as many as five portions, constituting a record for this train since it commenced to run; the 'Torbay Limited' was run in three parts, and the various portions of these trains conveyed in all nearly 5,000 passengers. Eighteen excursion trains were run from Paddington, on Friday, July 30, conveying 10,300 passengers. The provincial period excursions were also very well loaded, and the short-distance excursion traffic over the whole of the August Bank Holiday period was well above the average. On Sunday, August 1, seven half-day excursion trains were run to the Wye Valley district, Weston-super-Mare, and the Midlands, and conveyed a total of 3,500 passengers. On August Bank Holiday Monday the ideal weather conditions resulted in considerable passenger traffic between local stations, and large numbers of passengers were attracted from populous centres to adjacent seaside resorts. (*Great Western Magazine* 1926)

SWINDON WORKS

- ① Swindon Old Town
- ② Swindon Station
- ③ Railway Village
- ④ N°8 Carriage Paint Shop
- ⑤ N°7 Carriage Finish Shop
- ⑥ N°4 Carriage Body Shop
- ⑦ St Mark's Church
- ⑧ South Side Timber Sheds
- ⑨ Newburn House (CME Residence)
- ⑩ Main Line to Bristol & South Wales
- ⑪ Concentration Yard
- ⑫ Coal Stack
- ⑬ Sawmill Yard
- ⑭ North Side Timber Sheds
- ⑮ Weighbridge House
- ⑯ 'A' Wheel (AW) Shop
- ⑰ 'A' Erecting (AE) Shop
- ⑱ 'A' Machine (AM) Shop
- ⑲ Pattern Store
- ⑳ 'J' Shop Iron Foundry
- ㉑ 'V' Boiler Shop
- ㉒ Boiler Testing House
- ㉓ Tender Shop
- ㉔ 'X' Points & Crossings Shop
- ㉕ Machine Stores
- ㉖ Stock Shed
- ㉗ Locomotive Sheds
- ㉘ General Stores
- ㉙ 'B' Erecting Shop
- ㉚ N°15 Machine Shop
- ㉛ N°21 Wagon Shop
- ㉜ N°19 Carriage Shop
- ㉝ Cocklebury Sidings

1. Swindon Old Town
2. Railway Village
3. Swindon Station
4. Cocklebury Sidings
5. Water Sidings
6. Nº21 Wagon Repair Shop
7. Nº19 Carriage Repair Shop
8. Nº18 Stamping Shop
9. Nº17 Road Vehicle Shop
10. Nº15 Machine Shop
11. Nº13 Wagon Frame Shop
12. General Stores
13. Coaling Stage
14. Loco Yard Signal Box
15. 1871 Locomotive Shed
16. 1908 Locomotive Shed
17. Stock Shed
18. Brickyard Sidings
19. Remains of North Wilts Canal
20. Great Western Gas Works
21. Main Line to Gloucester
22. Rodbourne Road
23. Loco Yard Sidings
24. Nº8 Carriage Paint Shop
25. Nº7 Carriage Finish Shop
26. Works Main Offices
27. 'B' Erecting Shop
28. 'F' Shop Smithy
29. 'G' Shop Millwrights
30. Machine Stores

Oblique aerial images captured by Aerofilms Ltd, which started operating a De Havilland DH-9 aircraft from Hendon Aerodrome in 1919.

SHEPHERDING THE BRANCH LINE "CORNISH RIVIERA"

Acts of Parliament, Board minutes, surviving technical studies document the formal story of the establishment and expansion of the Great Western. However, these bland accounts provide little insight into the hard bargaining conducted among those of wealth and influence whereby the resources were marshalled to realise the dream of a London to Bristol railway. In turn, comparatively little survives to show how the administration of the grand venture developed the means of ensuring its efficient operation.

Much was learned from practical experience. Despatch of trains at regular intervals in the absence of any formal method of control was soon proven inadequate to protect a failed train on the open line. A combination of Government legislation, trial and error, improving technology and unfortunate experiences saw progressive improvements in operational control. Systems developed by the GWR and others were remarkably efficient and cost-effective in the pre-electronic age. Mechanical systems were long-wearing, simple, robust. Their reliability was sustained by a myriad of instructions and procedures enforced by ordinary railwaymen who took enormous pride in knowledge of those rules, and in their proper execution. There was a tacit and powerful partnership between management and the man on the ground (or in his signal box) that fulfilled the role of good shepherd in guiding each train to its destination.

Rules, regulations, instructions saw aggregation in the working timetables and staff rosters that governed train working and a brief summary of some measures that ensured safe passage of the 'Cornish Riviera' (the 'Limited') provide an insight into their effectiveness. The GWR's most prestigious service departed the capital at the time-honoured 10.30 am. From 1906 onwards, its journey west was by the Langport cut-off, and so it turned left at Reading West on to the Berks and Hants route.

Leaving Paddington, the Limited was belled from signal box to signal box with 'four beats' (per Regulation 1 of the 'Regulations for Train Signalling on Double and Single Lines'), the message being 'Is line clear for Express Passenger Train?'. Assuming all was well, that the clearing point was not fouled and that the section was indeed clear, the box in advance would turn its block to 'Line Clear' allowing continuation from box to box, block to block, through Ealing, Maidenhead, as far as Reading under the protection of 'four beats'. (Practical aspects of signalling procedures will be explored in later issues.)

At Reading, there was a change in this pattern. On the approach, Kennet Bridge Signal Box (approximately one mile to the east of the station) would determine the state of the section from there to Reading Main Line East Signal Box (at Old Junction) in the usual manner. A quarter of a mile beyond the station stood Reading Main Line West Signal Box, beside Basingstoke Line Junction (i.e. the connecting route southwards to the London & South Western Railway). In consequence of these movements the bell code from Reading East Main Line SB to its neighbour at West Main Line SB would be three-pause-one, describing the code for a branch passenger train. Thus for a short spell, the "Cornish Riviera Express" officially became a branch service!

Had the timetable always run strictly to plan and provided that there were no 'box to box' specials (extra trains, information about which was passed on from signal box to signal box), then the 'Cornish Riviera' could theoretically have been described by 'four beats'. However, this was used for any express passenger working regardless of destination, hence this was a planned arrangement. Further, the bells were never ignored making them faster than a telephone call. The late Reg Harvey, once of Reading East Main, recounted that the telephone was an instrument of last resort.

In this type of situation, a Southern Railway-type route code might appear to have been the answer, but this description described the route, without defining the train type e.g. express or stopping service. The GWR covered both aspects starting with the Summer 1934 timetable by use of three-digit train reporting numbers for principal services. Their purpose was to help identification by both signalling and platform staff. The knowledgeable would thereby know if a service was to schedule or running out of course. The down 'Cornish Riviera', the 10.30 am from Paddington was always appropriately No 130 under the three digit system.

Having negotiated Reading and joined the Basingstoke branch, the next signal box was at Oxford Road Junction which would have received the four-beat advice from Reading Main Line West. The same message would in turn be passed to Southcote Junction where the route divided three ways: - first left to the Coaley goods-only branch; straight on down to Basingstoke; right on to the Berks and Hants route proper which was officially

Where it all happened – the junction at Reading where the Berks and Hants route diverges to the left from the Bristol line. Reading motive power depot is immediately ahead. The view was taken looking westwards from Reading West Main Line Signal Box. The rear of the ground signals have been painted in a light shade, presumably as an early Health & Safety measure (the GWR's term 'Safety Movement' is really preferable). On the same theme, the *GWR Magazine* in 1926 had several pages devoted to safety in various operational areas including workshop practices, cartage, permanent way, and even the use of bicycles when travelling to and from work. Allowing for some track and signal changes, this scene altered little until provision of the flying junction for trains using the Berks & Hants route in recent years.

Full or empty? A loaded train of this length on the climb to Savernake would be beyond the capacity of even sturdy No. 6844 *Penhydd Grange* as 26 tank wagons plus a Passenger Brake Van can be identified, and there appears to be more behind. The location is near Southcote Junction and these empties are being worked back to the West Country over the Berks & Hants route. As a rule of thumb, an empty 6-wheeled milk tank wagon weighed about 14 tons and full it would be roughly double that figure which was not far short of a bogie coach. The weight of that part of the train which is in view is thus about 400 tons. (A loaded milk train could have say 10 tank wagons and a PBV, making for a legitimate 4-6-0-hauled short train as a modelling subject). The date of this photograph is unknown but it was probably late 1940s or early post-nationalisation.

WESTERN TIMES

defined as the main line at this location. The Limited would continue westward to Calcot and Theale under the four-beat code.

Regulations 3 and 4 provided another example of a bell code for a diverging train. 'Branch Freight Train – 1 pause 2' informed a junction signal box of a service for the branch and not the main line. An example was the code from Sandford to Radley, informing the latter location of the approaching Abingdon branch freight. Radley would change the code to three continuous beats 'Freight Train stopping at intermediate Stations' when sending on to Abingdon. (That there were none between Radley and Abingdon was irrelevant.)

During an extended and unofficial study of signalling procedures some decades ago, a comment made to every trainee signalman was 'always know what your next bell code should be so you know what to expect'. For this he would also have to be well acquainted with the timetable. But as an example a signalman would be immediately on suspicion if '2 pause 2 pause 1' (empty coaching stock) was received instead of four-beats denoting an expected express. Errors did occur although this was rare with experienced men. Pauses could be almost omitted in normal working although they were deliberately inserted if there was a new man or it was something unusual.

Another common operational feature was the use of banking engines on steep gradients, such as here on Dainton East. The Granges were versatile machines but it would have been more normal to use one of Newton Abbot's large prairies on this duty. The working methods for banking locomotives have recently been discussed among the editorial team. Breasting Dainton summit in the tunnel must have required careful control and co-operation between the two locomotive crews and the guard. A train of say 30 wagons would be traversing 1 in 37 up and then 1 in 36 down with the abrupt change interrupted only by a short level stretch. This would have yielded sudden changes between taut and loose couplings before ensuring firm control on the descent. It was a standard requirement for an unfitted goods trains to stop for the pinning down of brakes before a steep descent but dispensation to this rule could be granted with the approval of the District Inspector. Information would be welcome on the rules in force at Dainton and at the summit of Rattery/ Hemerdon banks. Can a retired railwayman help?

Left: This undated photograph at Old Oak Common was most likely taken on a Sunday judging by the row of panniers, most of which are out of steam. Also there is a line of larger locomotives standing in the left background with the closest a 2-8-0 Class 47xx, then two Halls and at least one Castle. On introduction of the modernised 0-6-0PT Class 8750, Nos. 8750 to 8774 were despatched to the London division. All but Nos. 8757/ 58/ 66/ 68/ 74 were allocated new to OOC which was home to No. 8763 for its entire career (October 1933 to September 1962).

Right: A case of recent history that has been lost is the covered ash shed. This example was one of the last, surviving at Didcot until demolition in 1964 due its poor condition. These structures were provided as a black-out measure at many depots during World War 2 to reduce the risk of glowing hot ash and clinker betraying the location to enemy aircraft. Another undated image but it might help that No. 6159 was a resident of Didcot from August 1960 until June 1965.

Bottom: One of the useful snapshot-type photographs taken to record the men. A note on the rear of this image advises that they are the fitting staff and perhaps the foreman at Machynlleth. Identities and the date are not recorded but early BR days seem likely as a shed code but no number plate has been attached to the smokebox door. Perhaps a relative might recognise someone? Is there a story to tell?

Over the years Bath Green Park witnessed a wide variety of visiting locomotives from other regions including ex-GWR types such as Moguls, Halls and Granges. This was particularly so after the transfer of Templecombe and Bath Green Park sheds to Western Region control in 1958 when pannier tanks and Collett 0-6-0s began to make an appearance. However, the arrival of a Castle class engine in June 1964 is believed to be the only occasion on which an example of these 4-6-0s graced the tracks of Bath's former Midland and Somerset & Dorset Joint station.

The 'Somerset & Dorset' Railtour was organised by the Home Counties Railway Society (HCRS) which had been formed in 1955 and was originally known as the Middlesex Loco Spotters Club. The name was changed in the late 1950s to the Home Counties Railway Club then in January 1963 to the Home Counties Railway Society.

Starting from Waterloo at 8.54 am, the special's motive power was Merchant Navy pacific No. 35002 *Union Castle* which took the train down the former LSWR mainline to Bournemouth Central where it arrived just over two hours later following a 5-minute water stop at Southampton Central.

The original intention had been to hand over at Bournemouth to the last two operational 2-8-0 Class 7Fs for a run up the Somerset & Dorset. However No. 53809 had been withdrawn two weeks earlier leaving only No. 53807 in service. Accordingly, the 2-8-0 was teamed up with another former S&D stalwart, Class 4F No. 44558, and with the 0-6-0 leading, the pair took the special up to Evercreech Junction. After taking on water there, they worked over the Highbridge branch thus providing the unusual spectacle of a 7F on that route.

Returning to Evercreech, the combination proceeded northwards to Bath where another

No. 7023 *Penrice Castle* carrying reporting No. X05 (the 'X' signifying a special train) and sporting an 85A Worcester shedplate stands at Bath Green Park, part of whose roof can just be seen in the background. This was prior to working a leg of the HCRS Special of 7 June 1964 which the locomotive would power as far as Gloucester. Notice the gentleman on the right with the loud hailer no doubt to be used to shepherd the railtour participants back to the train, at the same time the fireman checks to ensure that the headboard is firmly attached. Trespassing over the tracks and alighting from carriages where there was no platform were mostly tolerated in those days before the reign of Health & Safety circumscribed such activities.

unusual spectacle was encountered in the form of No. 7023. Arrival at Bath was 17 minutes behind schedule but some smart work saw the special away just 10 minutes down for the 50 minute run via Mangotsfield to stop at Gloucester Eastgate. The train then proceeded to Engine Shed Junction just to the north of Eastgate station where sister engine No. 7025 *Sudeley Castle* assumed command for the run back to Paddington via Swindon. The tour passengers arrived in the capital at 8:15 pm, fifteen minutes late having been drawn by five different locomotives over 370 miles. This locomotive was another last minute substitution as it had been intended to use No. 4079 *Pendennis Castle* but this too had been withdrawn a few weeks earlier following firebars incident on the high speed run of 9 May 1964.

No. 7023 had been released to traffic from Swindon Works in June 1949 and initially allocated to Cardiff Canton shed. In May 1958 it was modified with a four-row superheater and double chimney. In late 1963 the final scheduled Castle-hauled train was officially announced and No. 7023 was selected for this duty which was the 11.10 am from Worcester-Paddington on Saturday, 7 September 1963. The choice of *Penrice Castle* for this final train was perhaps unexpected as lifelong Worcester engine No. 7005 *Sir Edward Elgar* would have been the obvious choice in view of the local connections with the great composer. Possibly No. 7023 was in better mechanical condition and the authorities did not wish to repeat the embarrassment of No 4079's failure.

After this 'final' trip No. 7023 was placed in store at the rear of the Goods Shed at Worcester. However,

just before Christmas 1963, she returned to traffic for further use from Worcester on various main line duties until the following June when diesels finally reigned supreme. After handling the S&D tour *Penrice Castle* survived a little longer at Wolverhampton's Oxley shed, by then recoded 2B from 84B, to which she was formerly transferred on 27 June 1964 but continued to visit the Worcester area occasionally until withdrawal in February 1965. She then presented a rather forlorn sight on Oxley shed, shorn of nameplates and in company with other withdrawn members of the class, Nos. 7011 *Banbury Castle*, No. 7019 *Fowey Castle* and No. 7024 *Powis Castle*. The quartet was finally despatched in April to Cashmore's scrapyard at Great Bridge in the West Midlands town of Tipton.

No. 7023 was the third locomotive to carry the name *Penrice Castle*, the first being No. 5057 renamed *Earl Waldegrave* in 1937. The name was then transferred to No. 5081 but that lasted only until 1941 when No. 5081 became *Lockheed Hudson*. The structure after which No. 7023 was named lies on the Gower peninsula in South Wales and was built by the de Penrice family who were given land there in return for their part in the Norman Conquest. The castle was damaged in the English Civil War and a mansion was built adjacently in the 1770s. This is Grade I listed being considered amongst the finest country houses in Wales. Ironically the two withdrawn locomotives which should have been involved in the HCRS Railtour, Nos. 53809 and 4079, were lucky enough to escape the cutter's torch and at time of writing are based at the North Norfolk Railway and the Didcot Railway Centre respectively.

Two Newton Abbot division breakdown vehicles at Exeter. Closest is Tender Van No. 89 containing bunks and necessary messing facilities. Behind is Tool Van No. 141 effectively a travelling workshop. Such vehicles were often paired for long periods.

THE NEWTON ABBOT BREAKDOWN TRAIN

One facet of the operational railway scene that has seemingly received scant attention over the years is the essential role of the breakdown train. With the notable exceptions of Peter Tatlow's benchmark three-volume opus on *Railway Breakdown Cranes* (Noodle Books 2012/4 and Crecy 2018) and also *Railway Steam Cranes* by John Brownlie (privately published 1973), these unique and specialised vehicles seemed to avoid the literary and photographic spotlight, possibly due to the irregular and clandestine nature of their work. It is perhaps surprising to note that British Railways inherited 107 specialist breakdown cranes across its six regions, from a disparate range of manufacturers and designs.

The Great Western's contribution was typical in that barely any two of the larger running sheds could roster a complete breakdown train resembling anything that might be classed as standardised. Even the terminology employed was diverse with tool/ mess/ tender/ travelling/ riding all variously used to identify the usage of individual vans.

Looking specifically at the Newton Abbot division, the cranes and accompanying support vehicles were sited at Newton itself and in later BR(W) years at Plymouth Laira. In addition, breakdown vans (usually tool and riding) were allocated to Taunton, Exeter, Laira, St Blazey, Truro and Penzance. These were sufficient for a team of six to twelve men and equipment to be deployed to an incident across the districts, within 15 minutes of a call from the Traffic Department.

When the lifting jacks, chains and ramps contained within the tool vans were insufficient to deal with a derailment and for the more serious accidents, the divisional steam breakdown crane would be summoned. Newton Abbot received its first dedicated allocation around 1910, when Cowans Sheldon Standard 15-Ton Crane No 8 arrived from Swindon. Built in Carlisle in 1901 to works number

Cowans Sheldon 15-Ton Crane No 8 stands on the dedicated siding next to the Weighouse, with the Newton Abbot Works building behind. This late 1930s image shows the regular Churchward 2-6-0 coupled to the crane and its L15 match truck. *Unknown.*

From a similar vantage point at the northern end of Platform 1, this post-war view depicts newly arrived 36-Ton Ransomes & Rapier Crane No 3 standing with 6-wheel Tool Van No 114. This large 10-wheel crane unit was permanently accompanied by L11 Match Truck No W3 (DW3) and L10 Weight Tender No W3A (DW3A) just visible left and right respectively. *P W Gray Collection.*

2448T, this Mk.2 swan neck jib version of the company's successful design was originally designated as No 1 by the Great Western before being renumbered in 1909. It was paired with an 11' wheelbase diagram L15 Match Truck in 1914 and remained present at the shed until late 1963.

In 1936 No 8 was augmented by a second heavier vehicle in the form of ex-Rhymney Railway Cowans Sheldon 35-Ton crane No 9. Built in 1913 and the only one of its type acquired by the GWR, it arrived at Newton Abbot from Caerphilly and lasted until around 1948 when it moved to Worcester. The next notable event occurred when Ransomes & Rapier 36-Ton No 3 appeared at Newton Abbot shortly after the Second World War, on transfer from Worcester. Some allocation records suggest it did not arrive until 1956, but the photographic evidence indicates otherwise. This Ipswich built crane, works number B6113, was delivered to the GWR in July 1912 and ran with a diagram L11 bogie Match Truck and diagram L10 Weight Tender. It operated in south Devon until transfer to Landore shed in 1961. The last specialist steam breakdown crane allocated to Newton Abbot was a wartime Ransomes & Rapier 45-Ton variant, originally delivered to the Southern Railway in 1945. Numbered ADW151 by the Western Region, it arrived from Exmouth Junction in

August 1965 and remained at 83A until transfer to Laira in early 1972, thus bringing to a close the shed's association with steam powered cranes.

To complete the story, Great Western Standard 6-ton Steam Travelling Crane No 57, built at Swindon in 1919, should be mentioned. While not a dedicated breakdown crane, it operated with the Newton Abbot Locomotive Department between August 1936 and September 1950, primarily lifting components around the Works site, but it is known to have been used on other duties. Paired with a 19' wheelbase diagram L19 Match Truck, it returned to Newton Abbot for a second period between July 1961 and July 1968, this time in the service of the Mechanical & Electrical Engineers Department.

The breakdown vans at Newton Abbot were as varied as the cranes they supported. The first vehicles recorded were 6-wheel Tool Van No 114 built to Lot 446 in March 1904, 4-wheel Tender Van No 121 built to Lot 463 in October 1904, and 6-wheel Travelling Van No 126 of Lot 520 in October 1908. While the exact date of the trio's arrival is not recorded, it is known that Nos 121 and 126 moved to Laira in August 1924. In July 1938 Newton Abbot received the unique 4-wheel metal-bodied Mess Van No 103 which was built as a replacement

Opposite top: This scene shows how the steam cranes were also employed on permanent way duties. Ransomes & Rapier Crane No 3 is lifting concrete beams during the rebuilding of Tanners Road Bridge at Goodrington on 4 December 1955. Also present on this Sunday morning engineering task are Tool Van DW50 (a converted AA3 Toad), train engine No 6829 *Burmington Grange* and fellow Newton Abbot resident No 2809 hauling bolster wagons carrying the beams. *P W Gray* (PG 727).

Opposite bottom: On 26 April 1958 while hauling the 8.55 am Newton Abbot – Kingswear stopping train, No 7004 *Eastnor Castle* ran into the rear of a down goods train in Torre Station. The damage sustained required the attendance of Ransomes & Rapier 36-Ton Crane No 3 together with support vans DW103 and DW141. Initially parked in the Torre Goods Yard, the crane is being prepared for use with the jib and hook being lifted from the match truck. *P W Gray* (PG 1311).

Above: With the damaged *Eastnor Castle* now removed to the sidings in the background, No 3 gets to work lifting the wreckage of the goods train in order to clear the running lines. The Up line was reopened by late afternoon, but due to necessary track repairs the Down line remained closed until the following day. The Castle was recovered to Newton Abbot shed before eventual despatch to Swindon Works for repair. *P W Gray* (PG 1315).

vehicle to Lot 1302. Following the withdrawal of the original Tool Van No 114, a replacement arrived from Exeter shed during 1953, in the form of October 1908 built No 141 of Lot 579. This vehicle remained at the shed until transfer to Wadebridge in December 1964, before eventual preservation at the Severn Valley Railway. Additional Tool Van capacity was provided throughout the 1950s by DW 50, an early BR era conversion of a diagram AA3 Toad Brake Van, which featured an enclosed veranda and added side windows. In similar vein to crane No 57, another vehicle worthy of mention is 4-wheel Riding Van DW 215, which had been converted in 1946 from Dean diagram U4 composite passenger carriage No 747 of 1900 vintage. It was employed by the M & E E Department at Newton Abbot but supplemented breakdown operations on many occasions. It has survived in preservation on the South Devon Railway.

The livery of the cranes in Great Western days is open to conjecture, with dark grey and black both being cited. What is certain is that these vehicles were painted plain black by British Railways with pale straw lettering adorning the match trucks. Vans were GW brown with red ends until again repainted black by BR. Latterly, a General Instruction was issued by Swindon in the summer of 1959 to paint cranes and support vehicles red after overhaul. Newton Abbot Division was slow to respond to this directive, with the Laira Breakdown Train being the first so treated early in 1961. Some of the older cranes like Cowans Sheldon 15-Ton No 8 were to be scrapped still wearing black.

Newton Abbot had a dedicated siding for its breakdown cranes situated beside the 65 ft turntable and Weigh House which meant that they were easily viewed from the platforms at the north end of the station. It is therefore surprising that they were photographed infrequently, probably indicative of the lower regard in which less glamorous departmental rolling stock was held. The support vans were stabled nearby on a loop directly behind the down carriage sidings and were usually partially hidden from public gaze. This loop allowed locomotive access to both ends of the breakdown train to facilitate speedy despatch in either the Exeter or Plymouth directions. The dedicated standby locomotive was kept in permanent readiness for an emergency call and the link was diagrammed for a tender engine, although tank engines were occasionally used for incidents on the Torbay line. For many years Newton Abbot shed allocated a Churchward Mogul to the duty but Manor, Grange and Hall 4-6-0s were also used. It is noted that on one occasion, resident Castle Class No 5024 *Carew Castle* was used to haul the train to attend a derailment involving milk tankers at Totnes. Indeed, working the Newton Abbot Breakdown Train could certainly never be described as a routine duty.

Above: At the foot of Dainton Bank on Saturday 15 October 1960, Hall Class 4-6-0 No 4934 *Hindlip Hall* and Large Prairie 2-6-2T No 5183 were working westwards with Cranes Nos 3 and 8 plus Riding Van DW 215. The absence of the breakdown train mess and tool vans suggest this unusual consist was destined for a weekend engineering possession rather than an operating mishap. *P W Gray* (PG 2459).

For further detail on Breakdown Cranes the reader is referred to the excellent 'Railway Breakdown Cranes' series by Peter Tatlow published in three volumes.

Lower: In September 1961 Standard GW 6-ton Crane No 57 and Riding Van DW 215 were standing on the recently remodelled sidings alongside the Newton Abbot Works traverser. While officially allocated to the Mechanical & Electrical Engineers Department, both vehicles saw occasional use in support of breakdown operations. *Author's Collection.*

BOOK REVIEW

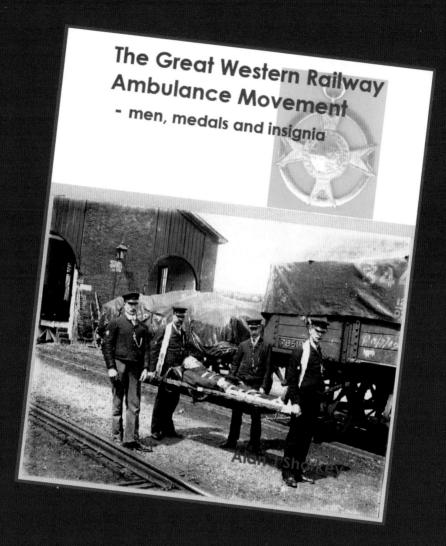

We corresponded recently with Alan J Sharkey who has produced a series of self-published books on the railways and their association with the St Johns Ambulance movement. Many will recall the stretchers with the emblem of St John on the woodwork while anyone who has studied the *Great Western Magazine* will recall the importance accorded knowledge of First Aid by both management and many of the staff. First aid equipment was readily accessible at stations and was also kept in guard's vans, at depots, and at other key locations. So far as the GWR is concerned, Alan has produced a 59 page print-on-demand title detailing the history of First Aid on the railway with examples of St Johns insignia, awards, and also interesting case studies. The cover picture certainly sold this work for the reviewer. Details from alansharkey@btopenworld.com .

Have you had a book on the GWR published recently? If so we would be happy to provide an objective review. Speak to your publisher and ask them to send a copy to the address on page 2.

A FEW CLOSED LINES

Above: Of all the closed lines in former Great Western territory, those around the area of the Wye Valley must surely be some of the most sorely missed. Ross-on-Wye station dated from 1855 as part of the Hereford, Ross and Gloucester company. Eighteen years later, it became a junction with the opening of the Ross and Monmouth route. Closed in stages starting with passenger services to Monmouth in 1959, passenger services over the HR&G line ceased in 1964. As was often the case, freight services continued for a period but were withdrawn in November 1965. In this image dated September 1966, all is moribund and the last trains have called.

Opposite: Two views from April 1965, the first south of Buckfastleigh near the site of Bulkamore Siding and then at Ashburton, the terminus of the original Dart Valley Railway. BR Western Region closed the line to passengers in November 1958, but seven years later it was still intact, largely due to strenuous efforts by dedicated enthusiasts to see this picturesque route restored as a heritage railway. Occasional trains did operate between Buckfastleigh and Ashburton but these activities ceased in 1971 with severance of that section to facilitate conversion of the nearby A38 trunk road to dual carriageway. Much of the route remains in place but devoid of track as does also Ashburton station itself. With all the usual facilities it has been described as the archetypal prototype of a GWR branch line terminus for modellers. The loss is also felt among the local community; there is a public house near the terminus called 'The Silent Whistle'...

Above: Christow on the Teign Valley line between Exeter and Heathfield, recorded in May 1963. Originally opened as a terminus from Heathfield in 1882, the line was extended north and east to Exeter in 1903. After a comparatively short life, closure to passengers came in 1958. Generally, the earlier a line opened the greater chance it had of surviving as the pioneer railways focussed on reaching the centres of greatest business potential. In more recent times, reinstatement of this line as an alternative connection between Exeter and Newton Abbot has been mooted as a diversionary route away from the vulnerable sea wall of the Dawlish-Teignmouth section. This suggestion recurs from time to time but does not seem to be high on the current list of priorities.

Opposite top: This was Kington in September 1965, recalling the days when a 'poke around' a closed station site would invariably reveal something the contractors had not recovered. In this case, it was the nameboard. This station was in use for 89 years and closed completely in 1964 although passenger services had ceased in 1955, so Dr Beeching cannot be blamed for that one! A model of the station as it appeared in the 1940s is displayed in the volunteer-run local history museum in Kington.

Opposite bottom: Winchester Chesil ("Cheeshill" as it was called), devoid of train and track in the Autumn of 1968. This was the southernmost outpost of the Great Western in Hampshire but had been transferred to the Southern Region consequent upon the regional boundary changes of 1950. This view is looking north towards Newbury, 27 miles distant and eventually Didcot another 17 miles further. Opened as a terminus in 1885, a connection with the LSWR Basingstoke-Eastleigh line two miles south in 1891 ended hopes of an independent route to Southampton. As with the ex-Midland & South Western Joint Railway route, this line was heavily used during World War 2 for which it was extensively upgraded in 1942. This investment was essential to cope with the extraordinary demands associated with D-Day but endowed the operators with excessive infrastructural costs in the context of reduced traffic following restoration of peace. Closure came in stages, between 1960 and 1962 to passengers and to freight between 1964 and 1966. Today, a multi-storey car park occupies the site.

PASSENGER DIVISIONS AND SUBURBAN SETS

Elsewhere in this issue there is an overview of the divisional structure through which the GWR managed its business. At this distance it is difficult to determine how much management autonomy was enjoyed at divisional level but differing means of identifying suburban train sets provide a clue. System-wide there was a preference to assemble non-corridor stock into fixed sets (not necessarily permanently coupled) for operational convenience and for creation of rosters to cater for predicted traffic levels. Most familiar was probably the pairing of N/ C Brake Composites that were widely, but not exclusively, designated as B-Sets. As an aside, despite their ubiquity the duplication of guard's, luggage, and first class accommodation would seem wasteful in such a short formation. Further, deployment on longer distance stopping country services might have made the absence of toilet facilities something of an *in*convenience·

By their nature, the range of suburban services was largely discrete to their respective divisions with minimal trespass onto the turf of another. It would seem from the table below that the "set" discipline was retained but application of the letter prefix and the actual composition could vary widely. For example, in the Birmingham Division a B-Set was formed of a pair of Brake Thirds with two Composites in between, all vehicles to be of 57' length. In this case it is speculated that the Set discipline was expanded to cope with platform limitations on particular routes. Nevertheless, it is not clear why Birmingham chose to designate a pair of Brake Composites as a D-Set.

The information laid out overleaf stemmed from a simple question directed to John Lewis around 20 years ago about what comprised an E-Set. John's very helpful response, drawn from the 1937/8 period revealed that this subject is actually far from simple.

Probably the best-known formation was the B-Set comprising a pair of non-corridor Brake Composites with the guard's or van section outwards. They were usually associated with rural duties and could be found working over quite long distances. Here 2-6-2T No 6149 has paused with a B-Set at Thame on the Oxford-Princes Risborough route on 19 August 1962. The angle of the photograph prevents identification of the Diagram but they seem to be of either late Collett or Hawksworth vintage. Passenger services over this line were withdrawn in January 1963. *R16251-610*

Set Type	London	Birmingham	Bristol	Exeter & Plymouth	Gloucester & South Wales
Suburban	VT/C/C/VT				
A (4-coach)	VT/F/C/VT				
A (5-coach)	VT/T/F/T/VT				
A		VT/C/C/VT(70')			VT/LavC/VT
B	BC/BC	VT/C/C/VT(57')	BC/BC	BC/BC	BC/BC
C	VT/T/F/LavC/VT	VT/T/C/T/VT			
D	VT/C/C/VT	BC/BC	VT/C/C/VT		VT/C/C/VT
E	VT/F/T/VT	BC/LavC/VT		BC/LavC/VT	
F		VT/T/C/VT			VT/T/C/VT
G	VT/T/C/Van	VT/T/C/VT			VT/T/C/VT
H	VT/LavC/VT		VT/LavC/VT		
K					VT/T/C/VT
M		VT/C/VT	VT/T/LavC/VT	VT/LavC/T/VT	VT/T/LavC/VT
U		VT/C/VT		VT/C/VT	

Notes

[1] Abbreviations: VT = Van Third (i.e. Brake Third); F = All First; C = Composite; Lav C = Composite with lavatory accommodation; T = All Third; BC = Brake Composite. Numbers in brackets define number of first class compartments within the vehicle.

[2] Details for Chester division were not available; Central Wales division apparently did not use the system at all

On 11 April 1955, No. 6156 was passing West Ealing on a down service comprising a formation that pre-war would have been designed a London A-Set. The first coach is a modernised Toplight Brake Third (Diagram D49 or D67; note that Diagram D53 built specifically for London suburban work had seven compartments and a shorter van section). The next vehicle is a BR Mark 1 All Third; that following is of GWR design origin and is probably a Composite as it was normal practice to place first class accommodation in the centre of a 5-car set. The fourth is obscured but the Brake Third at the far end looks also to be an ex-GWR Brake Third. *R5001-6100 (699)*

41

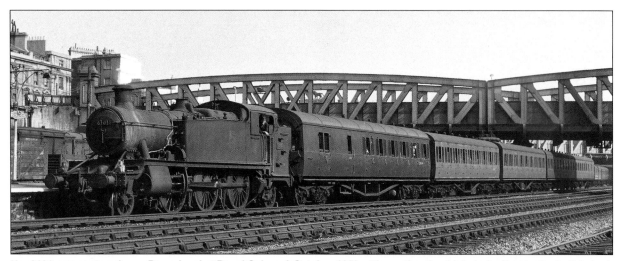

No. 6101 was captured on a Down local at Royal Oak on 3 October 1959 with another 5-vehicle train. Frustratingly, it is just not possible to identify the running number but the combination of end windows to the van section, flush guard's door, six compartments and position of roof ribbing suggests that the leading coach is a bow-ender Brake Third of Diagram D98 (built 1927/ 29). The next appears to be a flat ended 9-compartment All Third Diagram C66 (1934-6) although almost identical batches followed as Diagram C75 (1937-40). The centre coach appears to be a Hawksworth 9-compartment 63' E166 Composite (five First class and four Second class compartments). The final two seems to be 63' Hawksworth coaches also – a 10-compartment C83 All Third and a 6-compartment D132 Brake Third.

The purpose of the Heath Robinson pipework from the tank top of the 61 down to behind the steam pipe is unclear. Also this seems to be an unusual location at which to find a distinctly travel-worn 8-plank ex-private owner wagon in the goods train at the adjacent platform. *R14000-15099 (332)*

The variety implies sensible discretion in allowing divisions to fashion their formations in suit local demand patterns. However, photographic evidence suggests that set types were not necessarily switched to meet predicted peaks in demand. For example, the 2-coach B-set was the standard formation for almost all the Cornish branches throughout the year but was often augmented in the holiday season by attachment of a Third Class corridor or non-corridor "filler". A corridor All Third thus offered the oddity of a service providing toilet facilities that were denied to first class clientele.

Twice a year, coach working booklets were issued by divisions which defined the set designation plus the type and number of associated vehicles. Not only did this vary between divisions but also from period to period within a division. For this reason, the summary provided above should be treated with caution. Within the London division, the booklet identified the day's duties by a number that referred by letter to the vehicle set to be used and listed the actual services to be worked. Apparently, this Set number did not correlate to the numbering of local sets familiarly carried on the ends of the outer vehicles e.g. "London Division Train No 6" etc.

The most permanent formations seem to have been 2-coach B-sets which were usually close-coupled over short buffers. Pairs tended to remain monogamous with consecutive running numbers. Other formations were less disciplined and while the

pre-determined combination of coach types was adhered to, vehicles could be drawn from a variety of vintages, hence displaying differences in body styles. Non-corridor coach construction programmes tended to produce Brake Thirds, All Thirds and Composites with the intent of producing matched trains. However the accompanying photographs of 5-coach trains (A-Sets by the definition of 1937/ 8) in the London division in the 1950s and early 1960s reflect *ad hoc* re-marshalling.

The divisional booklets seem to have suffered a poor survival rate, presumably on account of their twice-yearly replacement cycle. Reader's loans for photocopying and prompt return would be most welcome.

Finally, use of the lesser-known set designations allows for some technical snobbery. One of the editorial team, whose modelling endeavours are based "somewhere in the Cotswolds on 6th June 1938", has assembled all the ingredients to scratch-build a Gloucester K-Set, as and when time (that familiar enemy) permits. This will be of the same vintage and thus body style throughout but will comprise vehicles from diagrams C66/ D117/ E156, so lengths will differ. For a supposed disciple of standardisation, the GWR's coach fleet provided some fascinating and at times bewildering variety.

Above: This view displays part of a Hawksworth D132 Brake Third W2762W. This diagram was among the last built to GWR designs. Introduced to service in May 1952, this coach was withdrawn in November 1963 yielding a shamefully short career. The well-groomed No. 6142 is passing Royal Oak on an Up empty stock working on 27 August 1960. *R15100-216*

Right: Prior to the DMU invasion, mainline local passenger traffic was largely handled by the combination of a 61xx 2-6-2T and a 5-coach set so here is something different that raises questions. Before introducing the well-known mainline articulated trains in 1925, the GWR attempted to improve the operating efficiency of suburban passenger trains by building three 6-coach non-corridor articulated trains. They were high density units so designed to minmise the tare weight. Each set comprised two each of Brake Third (Diagram D93 – 60 seats each); Third (Diagram C53 – 80 seats each); Composite (Diagram E126/ E133 – 40 First Class seats/ 20 third class seats each). They worked in the London division until 1939 and were then transferred to Bristol and South Wales. Longer lived than the mainline sets, a member of the editorial team saw one working out of Bristol Temple Meads about 1959.

This suburban working was photographed leaving Goring on the Down slow on 13 May 1955, hauled by No. 5026 *Criccieth Castle.* A 4-cylinder 4-6-0 on such a mundane service seems unusual as does the use of this set which apparently had been transferred away some 16 years earlier. Further, the GWR built one train made as a pair of three articulated vehicle sets (VT + T + C/ C + T +VT) while the other two were six vehicles articulated throughout. No 5026's train was one of the latter but the original composition (VT + T + C + C + T + VT) has been modified. The first three coaches are VT + C + T while the next two are partially obscured but the final vehicle is another VT (followed by what seems to be an ex-SR Utility van). Articulation evidently did not prevent re-ordering the set composition. *R5001-6100 (1063)*

43

MODERN TRACTION

Above: Sometimes referred to as 'razor edge' vehicles in consequence of the cab-end body styling, one of the later GWR-design diesel railcars was at Tenbury Wells on 3 June 1961. There were variations between the earlier railcars which were somewhat experimental in nature but Nos 19-33 of which this vehicle was an example could be regarded as a standard design. Intended for branch line services, they were geared for a maximum speed of 40 mph (two with dual ratio gearboxes could manage 60 mph). They had seating accommodation for 48 plus a luggage and guard's section. Mechanically, they followed the earlier "Flying Banana" series with two engines but most importantly were equipped with drawgear as introduced experimentally with vehicle No 18. With an ability to haul a trailing load of 60 tons, they enjoyed significantly greater operating flexibility. Folklore has it that some drivers would carry a bucket with them to pick up bits of the machine when failures occurred, and sometimes they just ran on one engine so as to keep the second in reserve. Nevertheless mileage-wise, they gave a good account of themselves. As an example, Railcar No. 25 covered 420,00 miles between construction in September 1940 and December 1950.

Opposite top: As a comparison, No. 8 was one of the early 'streamlined' diesel railcars. In this undated view at Swindon it has clearly been out of service for some time having been withdrawn in January 1959. The nickname 'flying banana' was appropriate for this series given their curvaceous lines and original chocolate and cream livery. The present condition makes for a sad comparison with No. 11 of the same series seen new at Salisbury elsewhere in this issue. Completed in March 1936, No. 8 was the first of a batch of ten and the size of this order reflected general satisfaction with the preceding seven examples in this pioneering project. They came in three forms: Nos 8, 9, 13-16 provided seating for 70 passengers; Nos 10-12 sat 63 passengers but also provided toilet accommodation; No 17 followed the same external body contours but had no windows nor seating, serving as a parcels only vehicle. No. 18 was built as a specific branch-line car but although sucessful the design was not replicated. Alongside, saddle tank No. 1361 (withdrawn in May 1961) is standing adjacently while also in view is a new Swindon built Inter-City unit.

Opposite bottom: The Railway Enthusiasts Club of Farnborough 'Devon Rambler' railtour of 11 April 1959 at Plymouth North Road in the course of its St Davids – Lydford – Laira Yard – Friary – Yealmpton – Turnchapel Tunnel – St Budeaux – Millbay – Dawlish – Exeter St Davids programme. The design of the first generation DMUs meant that most allowed passengers to have a reasonable forward (or backward) view of the line, provided that the driver was content to work with the black concertina window blind behind him left up. Some were less accommodating as they did not welcome nosey passengers looking over their shoulders as they drove. Vehicle No. 51090 was a Driving Motor Second of a 3-car Cross Country DMU with two B.U.T (A.E.C.) 150 bhp 6-cylinder engines, introduced by Gloucester Railway Carriage and Wagon Co in 1958 and later classified Class 119. The other two vehicles in the set were a Trailer Buffet Second and a Driving Motor Brake Composite

Opposite top: With so much more around of greater interest, the compiler admits he never took much notice of first generation DMUs but believes that this is a 3-car suburban set built by Pressed Steel (readers' corrections will be welcome). The unit (with destination blind set for Newton Abbot) is standing on the siding that served the quay facilities at Kingswear (for Dartmouth). Presumably it was being kept out of the way as the month is September 1960 and this cramped terminus would have still been busy handling long distance services. On the opposite platform is a starting signal with 'cash register', the latter only ever installed where train speeds were 25 mph or less; departure from a terminus would certainly apply. The stock for a steam service is standing behind in the bay platform. The "blood and custard" coach is a Diagram C67 Collett flat ended All 3rd built between 1934 and 1936 . This series formed part of the last deliveries of "traditional" stock before introduction of the larger window more modern style, generically known as "Sunshine" stock. The maroon-liveried coach to the right would seem to be one of the latter type.

Opposite bottom: Kingswear (for Dartmouth) from another angle with a 3-car Gloucester R C & W Cross Country DMU (later designated Class 119) arriving at the head of another 2 or 3 car set. The year is 1963 and there are signs of change. The DMU has acquired a yellow front warning panel and four digit alpha-numeric headcodes are now in use. A Beyer Peacock diesel-hydraulic "Hymek" is at the other platform, awaiting departure. Any remaining steam usage is clearly limited as there is a coating of rust on the line on the road leading to the turntable.

Above: The 'Blue' Pullmans were forerunners of the High Speed Trains but only so far as being a multiple unit train with a power car (engine) at each end. The similarity really stopped there as the Pullman service – one can hardly call it 'Blue' in the reversed white and blue livery – was a luxury train for which a supplement was payable. The concept of the 'Blue Pullman' trains dated back to the Modernisation plan of 1955 with the idea of a luxury service operating between major centres. In the event only five trains were built, two six-car sets for the London Midland Region working between Manchester and London (St Pancras) from July 1960 and three eight-car sets for the Western Region; Bristol - Paddington, and Wolverhampton and Paddington from September of the same year. The third WR train was initially kept as a spare but came into regular use from September 1961 when it replaced the steam hauled 'South Wales Pullman'. Livery was Nanking Blue relieved by a white band running the length of the train along the window line. From 1966 electrification of the West Coast Main Line and the inauguration of an electric Manchester Piccadilly to Euston service meant the end of the diesel service on the LMR and all five sets were then concentrated on the WR. Attempts were made to effect full utilisation but these were never really successful, the best that could be achieved the running of a 12-car Pullman between Bristol and Paddington using the two former LMR sets now modified to operate in multiple; the additional jumper attachments gaining the sets the 'tear drop' soliloquy from some observers. With air conditioning becoming standard in ordinary stock and faster services available without the payment of a Pullman supplement the end was inevitable and this came in May 1973. Despite efforts to preserve one set all were scrapped after just over 12 years' service.

Opposite top: An unidentified 'Warship' in original green livery passing through Swindon in April 1962. Slightly unusual is the position of the signal arms to the rear, a circumstance that is not explained.

Opposite bottom: A pair of North British Locomotive Co Type 2 diesel-hydraulic (later Class 22) leaving Lostwithiel on a down train in September 1960. These "baby Warships" were an interesting attempt at a flexible machine equally capable of economically handling branch and local trains but with ability to handle main line services when working in multiple, as seen here. The type suffered reliability issues and although BR Western Region displayed foresight in negotiating rigorous after-sales support from the manufacturers, this was of no value following closure of North British in 1962. Modernisation of the Western Region was a gradual process under BR, as for example the locomotive(s) at the head of the train may have changed but the rolling stock and infrastructure remained unaltered.

Above: An unidentified Warship Class D8xx was standing at St Blazey on a frosty day in December 1960. The accompanying notes refer to a china clay service bound for Fowey docks but this does not accord with the subject train which appears to consist exclusively of closed vans. A train of china clay hoods could certainly be found standing at his point awaiting the road to either Fowey or Par docks. This would seem more likely to be a rake of empty wagons waiting to take the Par loop and proceed eastwards up the Cornish main line. St Blazey depot was home to a variety of locomotives engaged on freight work, probably including the 0-6-0PT Class 57xx standing in the yard, out of steam as witness the frost on the tank.

49

It was inevitable that accidents and incidents would occur on the railway although the Great Western enjoyed an enviable safety record, as was commented upon more than once by the Board of Trade's Inspecting Officers. Much of this was down to provision of the Automatic Train Control system but the company's reputation preceded introduction of that pioneering system. However, there were occasions when the GWR was not so fortunate although serious accidents were few before 1948; Shrivenham in 1936 and Norton Fitzwarren in 1940 were notable exceptions.

It would have been impossible to operate a railway without 'incidents' as opposed to serious accidents such as with shunting, slow speed collisions, and minor derailments. To cope with the latter category, re-railing ramps were strategically placed around the system, with their locations noted in the General Appendix to the Working Timetable. In circumstances where more robust repair was needed, breakdown cranes and associated vehicles were stationed at the principal depots.

As an example of safe working practices, Paddington figured in just eight reported incidents in the period 1840 to 1929. There was then a 54-year gap until a diesel engine overturned on the station approaches in 1983, outside the period covered by this publication. These events were termed 'Reported Accidents' i.e. where an investigation was conducted by an Inspecting Officer from the Board of Trade. (Applying the same criteria for that period, incidents sustained at other termini were Euston [11], Kings Cross [23] and Waterloo [23]).

Information contained in accident reports can be interesting from at least two perspectives. Firstly, where a full report still exists, it can be instructive about train formation and operating procedures in the relative period. Secondly considering the vast number of trains that arrived at and departed from

Standard Goods or 388 Class was introduced in November 1866 during Joseph Armstrong's regime at Swindon. When production ceased in October 1876, there were 310 of the class in service. Although intended as goods locomotives, they found work on passenger services so the use of unlucky No. 238 as stand-in for a failure would not have excited particular comment. The numerical size of Class 388 marked a change in standard gauge 0-6-0 policy as previously the largest had been the 30 members of the celebrated "Beyer" Class 322 of 1864/ 6. The tradition was maintained by the 260-strong Dean Goods that followed in 1883. The Standard Goods remained largely intact until mass withdrawals in the 1919-21 period when they were replaced by new Churchward Class 43xx 2-6-0s. They had been allocated throughout the GWR system but after 1921, survivors largely congregated in the Wolverhampton Division. The type became extinct on withdrawal of No 1094 (built November 1870) in March 1934. For a modest goods locomotive, the condition of No. 238 is remarkable to modern eyes but in an era when labour was cheap and plentiful, there were plenty of cleaners on hand to keep it pristine, and to burnish dome and safety valve bonnet. The elaborate lining above the footplate is noteworthy, a practice that died out in the Great War for more humble machines. No 238 had four changes of boiler during its career, the last being a saturated Belpaire boiler fitted February 1910. It was withdrawn in March 1922.

Standard Goods No. 883 was built in January 1874 but unlike No. 238 underwent only one change of boiler with the fitting of a newer Type S2 in June 1894. Withdrawals of the class commenced in the Spring/ Summer of 1904 and No 883 was one of the first to go in either April or May that year (there are several variations in recorded dates for this class). This photograph gives the impression that space was in short supply. An oil can is perched on the handrail just in front of the cab. A bucket has been suspended on the side of the tender, apparently from a transversely placed fire iron, just in front of the rear tool box . However, shortage of room is most apparent with the manner in which coal has been stacked high and with care to prevent its dislodgement. Platelayers presumably learned to keep a weather eye out for flying debris from the tenders of passing trains. The rivet line in the tender side that descends in a gentle gradient from the rear and then concludes with an arc curve down to running plate level describes the division between the coal and water spaces. The profile reflects an early attempt at a self-trimming style and the limited capacity explains why coal had to be stacked so high. Between 1855 and 1876, 463 of these sandwich-framed standard tenders were constructed for use with both passenger and goods locomotives. The wheelbase was originally 6' 0" + 6' 0" but changed to 6' 2" + 6' 10" later and the water capacity was either 1780 or 1800 gallons. Coal capacity does not seem to have been recorded but presumably depended on the skills of firemen and coal-stackers. This locomotive and No. 238 in the preceding view appear to be in the 1840-1881 period livery which comprised boiler cladding, cab, and tender sides in holly green (described as dark green/ blue); black boiler bands edged with two thin white lines; lining on cab and tender as two thin white lines; sandbox as for boiler cladding but edged black with single thin white line; outside frames chocolate brown with single red lining which feature is rarely discernible in photographs.

Paddington over the 1840-1929 period, the actual number of reported incidents was very small. Doubtless there were other incidents that went unreported, having been resolved through internal investigation and for which no paperwork survives. However, the following incidents were regard as sufficiently significant for a formal Enquiry although some surviving records are frustratingly sparse:

19 February 1840. Derailment, no other details

15 November 1840. Rear collision, six injuries

21 July 1874. No details given

25 July 1887. Buffer stop collision involving an excursion from Exeter that comprised 20 coaches with a break-van (sic) at each end plus a milk van at the tail end. The train was fitted with continuous brake but this was not in use. Speed was controlled by the tender brake only as the train ran into the

station. Knowing that the train was very long, the driver intended to pull as far forward as possible at Platform 10 but as he approached the buffer stop he realised the tender braking power was insufficient. By then there was no time to apply the engine's vacuum or steam brake; the latter would in any event have caused the coaches to rebound against the tender buffers. The engine hit the buffer stop at about 1 mph. and fourteen passengers were slightly hurt. The Inspecting Officer reported that the train was running late and had already paused at Westbourne Park for ticket collection. It might thus be assumed that the train ran slowly from that point to the terminus which could explain the reliance solely on the tender brake. The locomotive's identity was not recorded.

18 September 1888. On this occasion an arrival at Platform 2 collided with a stationary vehicle. Entering the platform, the driver discovered that the stopping distance had been reduced by a carriage

Built in April 1871, No. 1109 was another Standard Goods that had a comparatively short career. It was re-boilered in May 1886 and November 1903, and withdrawn in June 1913. Cleanly presented, this engine's lining is more muted than the preceding pair as the boiler bands are in the 1881-1906 period livery where thin orange lines have replaced the white. The prominent front sand box appears unlined. The Roscoe-type lubricator behind the chimney was a standard fitting that was dropped with boilers built after 1892.

No. 805 appears to have a similar livery style to that of No. 1109 although in this case faint lining can be seen on the sandbox. This engine was built in January 1874 and had two changes of round-topped boiler (in December 1889 and February 1901), and finally it received a saturated Belpaire version in April 1914. It was an early candidate for the post-war cull being withdrawn in December 1919. As with most class members, it is carrying a re-railing jack on the front running plate. The headlamps have prominent white diamonds on their sides which were intended to hang sideways during daylight to make the headlamp code clearer. Lamp codes changed over the years – by those applying in 1883, that on No 805 would appear to denote a train using the Relief Lines between London and Slough. For students of early signals, the slotted stop signal beside the locomotive is worthy of study.

truck that had been left adjacent to the buffer stop. The motive power was an unidentified single wheeler in charge of a long train comprising eleven 8-wheel and seven 6-wheel coaches, all continuously braked. Five passengers were injured, all of whom were believed to have left their seats prior to disembarking. Col Rich, Inspecting Officer, regarded the following factors as relevant to the incident: (i) The train had been running late (ii) The load was too heavy for the locomotive (iii) The driver had been continuously on duty for 14 hours which was considered excessive. It might be inferred that the driver had had to cope with an underpowered locomotive on a heavy train, and that tiredness had impaired his judgement.

9 August 1920. Buffer stop collision, resulting in derailment and collision with station structure. Two injuries reported.

12 January 1921. Rear collision, resulting in derailment and collision with structure. No injuries reported.

24 July 1929. Buffer stop collision, resulting in derailment and collision with structure. No injuries reported.

In none of these cases is there any record of who was held responsible and what action was taken against them.

A more serious accident occurred on 18 July 1898 involving 0-6-0 No 238. The location was near Acton and so not included in the list above. The train involved was the 4.15 pm Up passenger service from Windsor to Paddington comprising eleven coaches:- one 6-wheel van, nine close-coupled 4-wheel coaches, and one bogie brake composite vehicle.

The accident was caused by the complete fracture of the right hand connecting rod whereby the severed section adjacent to the big end flailed round and pierced the firebox. The footplate was immediately enveloped in steam and boiling water. Driver Walter Peart and Fireman Henry John Lances Dean either jumped or were blown from the footplate. Both men were taken to hospital but succumbed to their injuries the following day.

The automatic vacuum brake was subsequently found to have played its part. On examination, the regulator was still open but the broken connecting rod had severed the brake pipe, thereby destroying

The tender attached to No. 1088 is significantly different from the preceding examples being fitted with the revised wheelbase of 6' 2" + 6' 10". Also the restricted coal capacity has been partly redressed by the fitting of two coal rails above the side and end body panels. It carries another hefty load of fuel but in this case the presence of the coal rails has allowed stacking with less discipline than was evidently applied in the earlier scenes. Coal rails and side extensions on tenders of this vintage could only partially ease the capacity limitations imposed by mounting the springs on the running plate. Later designs with springs on the outside frames above the axleboxes allowed significant increases in both coal and water capacities. This locomotive was built in October 1870 and reboilered with a Wolverhampton Type W3 boiler in March 1884. It was an early recipient of a saturated Belpaire boiler in December 1902 which it carried until withdrawal in June 1920.

the vacuum and bringing the train to a halt 858 yards from where the failure had occurred. No passengers were injured and there was no damage to any other part of the train.

Investigation of the scene revealed the first mark on the permanent way, caused by the rush of steam, was 352 yards east of Acton West signal cabin (sic) and that these marks extended for about 300 yards. The first 150 yards of this distance also revealed marks on the sleepers made by the broken connecting rod.

Col Marindin, inspecting officer, was thorough in his investigation. He reported that No 238 had been built at Swindon in 1867, rebuilt in 1885 and 'thoroughly repaired' (overhauled) in October 1897 since when it had covered 25,916 miles. In total, it had travelled 329,416 miles run since 1885. As a member of the Standard Goods or 388 Class it had

been designed for express freight service, but was considered quite suitable for passenger duties. More information is provided on No 238 in the caption to the adjacent photograph.

In his evidence to the Enquiry, Guard William Jarrett stated that the train was running on time and with about 27 inches of vacuum showing on the gauge in the rear brake compartment. Just after passing Acton West Signal Box and running at about 50 mph, there was suddenly a lot of steam around the train. He looked out but could not see anything although even at the far end of the train he could feel the heat and hear a crackling sound. Realising that something was wrong, he went to apply the vacuum brake but found that this was already doing its job.

With the train stationary, the Guard and two other railway employees quickly made their way to the engine but all commented 'it was dead' meaning there was no fire and that the crew were missing. Meanwhile Alfred Rogers a fitter employed at Westbourne Park shed was a passenger in the following service that had been forced to stop behind the disabled train. He was asked by the Acton station master to examine the beleaguered engine. He found that the right hand connecting rod was broken in two places. One fracture was about three inches from the flat part of the big end and the other fracture was 13 inches from the first. Rogers secured the big end to make it safe for moving and tied up the long section to the slide bar.

More interesting was the evidence of James Barfield who was described as 'a running shed fitter' also from Westbourne Park. He stated that his duty together with others, "…is to examine and put right defects on engines at Paddington". No 238 had been previously reported as requiring attention to the right hand big-end on 30 May. Upon examination this was confirmed and Barfield closed the brasses and 'made everything all-right'. At the same time he looked over the rod and there was nothing apparently wrong. Barfield then observed "Of course my examination was not so critical as one if the engine had been at Swindon for general repairs, but I don't think there can have been an outward crack showing. I have seen the rod since the accident and at the place where the first fracture took place there is a bad flaw extending over about half the thickness of the rod. Apparently, this was an internal flaw and was not showing outwardly on 30 May."*

John Armstrong (of the renowned GWR Armstrong dynasty) who was Divisional Locomotive Superintendent at Paddington spoke next, and was both factual and defensive in his evidence. Factual in describing the history and dimensions of No 238 and defensive in his belief that he did not think the defect could have been seen unless the rod had been taken down and minutely examined. Further, even if the defect did exist when the engine was last at Swindon the previous October, it "…must have been a very minute internal flaw." He confirmed that in his 15 years at Paddington he had only previously experienced two broken connecting rods. Armstrong had apparently managed to speak to Driver Peart in hospital who mentioned that his leg had been cut by the outside rod as he tried to get off the engine.

Next came Alfred Attwood who was the Chief Locomotive Foreman at Westbourne Park running shed. He stated he was in charge of 130 engines at the shed. He spoke highly of Driver Peart whose role was described as a 'spare man' – later better known as being a driver in the 'spare link/gang'. There was similar praise for Fireman Dean. Attwood referred to the engine that would otherwise have been rostered to the train, 2-4-0 Class 3232 No 3250 which had previously broken down at Trowbridge and in consequence had remained there. As no other 2-4-0 was available, No 238 was selected for the duty. Attwood also stated that the engine had been in use the previous day with a 'heavy fast (Henley) special from Maidenhead'. Attwood commented he had spoken to Peart after he had booked on duty and "passed the time of day" with him.

Clearly something had also been said elsewhere for Attwood made a specific comment, "There is absolutely no ground whatsoever for the statement that Driver Peart made any objection to the engine, and Driver Philpott (who drove No 238 the previous day) has volunteered a statement to me since the accident that he believed it to be in good order in every respect."

Similar non-contentious evidence was given by the Assistant Foreman and also the cleaner who had worked on the engine prior to it leaving the sheds.

In his conclusions Col Marindin summarised the evidence and paid tribute to Driver Peart who, while probably travelling with his hand on the brake anyway, had managed to pull this to 'full-on' as he left the footplate. His summary confirmed that the flaw probably did not extend to the surface of the connecting rod and consequently would not have been visible. "…unless there was some carelessness, which I do not believe possible in an establishment such as Swindon….I have come to the conclusion that the accident was one which could not have been prevented, and that there is no reason to impute blame to anyone."

Three other incidents involving boiler/ firebox explosions caused by various means are known at locations that later became part of the GWR. These were at Plympton in 1849, Totnes in 1860, and finally on the Rhymney Railway system at Cardiff in 1909.

*X-ray examination of components to detect potential flaws was not widespread until the 20th century whilst the first medical use of X-rays was reported in 1895.

None of the six photographs in this series is dated but No. 794 depicted here is in later condition. The preceding locomotives were carrying the Type S2 boiler but this engine is fitted with the more modern Type S4, which was carried from October 1902 until September 1909. This presents a tidier appearance than the others in this series with injectors, associated pipework and clack boxes no longer visible. The re-railing jack has been remounted horizontally on the running plate in front of the cab. Evidence of wear is apparent in the strengthening patches rivetted to the frames around the leading and driving axleboxes and also on the forward part of the tender frame. Although partly out of shot, the tender appears to be the later 6' 2" + 6' 10" wheelbase version. The coal capacity has been further improved by the fitting of metal plating behind the coal rails. The life histories of most of the Standard Goods were, well, pretty standard i.e. initially goods working throughout the GWR that evolved into a degree of mixed traffic work on slower, lighter passenger trains. However, 25 of the class were called up for military service in the Great War. Initially, six were sold to the UK Government in November 1915 but then repurchased by the GWR in March 1916. No. 794 was one of the group involved in those transactions, the purpose of which has not been explained. No. 794 had acquired a saturated Type B4 Belpaire boiler by the time it was part of a batch of six sold in August 1916 to the Railway Operating Division (together with Nos 508 & 1100 which had also been explained. No. 794 had also been overrun by Axis forces. Eight more of the class were sold to the ROD in May 1917 and another eight in September 1917. Of the Serbia which was impossible as by then that country had been overrun by Axis forces. Eight more of the class were sold to the ROD in May 1917 and another eight in September 1917. Of the 22 that were despatched for overseas service in the Mediterranean theatre, eight were lost at sea in the English Channel when their ship was torpedoed (all of the May 1917 block purchase). It is believed that the remaining 14 reached the Salonika Front in northern Greece. Of these, four were later sold to the Ottoman (Aidan) Railway after the war, four remain unaccounted for, and six were returned to the GWR in April 1921. No 794 was one of the six that made it home but its condition combined with the cull of the class then under way meant that its life expectancy was limited. It was withdrawn in December 1921.

JOHN ARMSTRONG

Having mentioned John Armstrong earlier in this issue, it is appropriate to provide a précis of his biography, This is drawn from Chapter 9 of *The Armstrongs of the Great Western* by Harry Holcroft.

The second son of Joseph Armstrong, John was born at Chester on 27 August 1851. He was one of nine children although two siblings died before reaching adulthood which was not unusual in those times. He was educated at Tettenhall Proprietary School, Wolverhampton which he attended as a boarder from age 13 following his father's move to take charge at Swindon.

On leaving school at 16, he entered Swindon Works as a pupil under his father and later worked in the Drawing Office. He completed his pupillage about 1872 but records of his career do not seem to have survived for the next 5-6 years. Joseph Armstrong a great family, company and social patriarch in the very best Victorian sense died suddenly of a heart attack in 1877 and was succeeded by William Dean. John was appointed Assistant Divisional Locomotive Superintendent of the Swindon Division that same year. Four years later at the age of 31 he was promoted to Divisional Locomotive Superintendent, Paddington Division where he would remain until retirement.

Before Old Oak Common was opened in 1906, the principal locomotive depot was at Westbourne Park which actually comprised two sheds. One was the original broad gauge depot (which had replaced a circular wooden building at Bishops Road). According to Holcroft, the BG shed was a large structure with dimensions of 650 feet x 71 feet and four parallel roads. The standard gauge shed which stood alongside initially consisted of two bays, each containing three roads with overall dimensions of 135 feet x 90 feet size. By extended northwards in 1873 its accommodation was doubled. Four years earlier in 1873 mixed gauge had been laid in the broad gauge shed thus mirroring the change that was effecting the whole system.

John Armstrong's duties included responsibility for the Royal Train used by Queen Victoria when visiting Windsor and he always rode on the footplate of the engine used for these duties. Journeys between Paddington and Windsor were commonplace but royalty

John Armstrong M V O.

57

also made longer journeys such as on *26* June 1895 when the Queen ventured by train to Highclere to stay at the nearby Castle.

Holcroft related the following tale from one of the Windsor journeys. "On one occasion the emergency bell on the engine rang, and when the train came to rest Armstrong descended from the footplate and walked back to find the cause. On approaching the royal saloon, Queen Victoria herself appeared at an open window and commanded "Drive on, it's all right." At the conclusion of the journey, Armstrong noticed that John Brown, the Queen's attendant, was looking very crestfallen. It appeared that he had pulled the communication cord in a spirit of bravado when drunk, and had been severely reprimanded by the Queen in consequence." A further tale again at the expense of the Queen during Armstrong's tenure may be told, again in Holcroft's words: "Queen Victoria was very fussy, and complained that her chair in the royal saloon was too high; and then after it had been lowered, it was too low. After about half a dozen alterations, the complaint was repeated, but nothing further was done for the next occasion. This time Her Majesty said the seat was then to her satisfaction!"

Armstrong continued to supervise the Royal trains including those involving the funerals of Queen Victoria (1901) and King Edward VII (1910). He also oversaw the trains in connection with the coronation of King George V. From 1914 onwards, in his offices at the south east corner of the new Old Oak Common depot he oversaw provision of locomotives for troop, munitions, and hospital trains plus those needed for normal services. On 28 September 1916 he was in charge of the royal train when King George V visited troops on Salisbury Plain (the precise destination is not recorded (Patney, Tidworth, or perhaps Codford?). On learning of Armstrong's impending retirement two days later following circa 50 years' service, he was summoned by his Majesty and questioned about his time with the GWR. This was soon followed by appointment as a member of the Royal Victorian Order (for distinguished personal services to the Monarch) at Buckingham Palace.

On retirement he continued what had been a busy and eclectic life, ranging from Methodism, the Temperance Union, tennis, and travel. Holcroft summed him up: "He was always serenely composed and reflected the perfect setting of his home life (where he lived with his wife Caroline [nee James], a son and three daughters), a man of high character, varied talents and rare personal qualities.".

John Armstrong was widowed in 1925 and three years later his own health began to fail so restricting his activities. He died in 1931 and is buried in Acton Cemetery.

(We have found no apparent close relationship between John Armstrong and W Y Armstrong who was concurrently the GWR's New Works Engineer.)

Above: King George V and Queen Mary inspecting huts on Salisbury Plain, c1916.

Opposite: John Armstrong would witnessed the last years of the broad gauge. He is believed to be on one those stood in front of the engine in the well-known view of the last broad gauge train to leave Paddington in 1892. This recently located broad gauge view shows *Swallow*, a member of the Iron Duke class and reputed to have been one of the last board gauge engines in steam being used for shunting stock at Swindon.

"Stand aside!" was a once common cry by station porters, especially on crowded platforms during the holiday season so let us take a few minutes to consider the Holiday Line's humblest of vehicles.

Allowing that many railways were built primarily for goods traffic, and that from early times passengers expected to be able to take luggage (or in some cases their own carriage, but that is outside the scope of this article), there was a need to facilitate that traffic.

In the absence of photographs of the first years, there are only a few contemporary lithograph type illustrations to show how passengers' baggage was moved to and from the train. It would seem that luggage barrows, sack trucks and the like, had a hard life, as few early examples appear in later photographs. One type that is clearly depicted is a single wheel barrow. This type resembled old fashioned market barrows being quite long, lightweight, and presumably made by the same manufacturers. A more robust and compact version of these ungainly devices was to be found across the GWR system from Victorian times and into the 1970s.

Left: The typical GWR single wheeler, with four spoke wheel. In BR days, many of these were fitted with a single five spoke wheel. This example was at Llangwril in 1967. Unwieldy when empty, your author can vouch for how difficult they were to manoeuvre, particularly across uneven surfaces and platform ramps. When loaded, they must have been decidedly challenging.

Bottom left and opposite page top left/ right: For heavier loads, particularly with the advent of milk churns, a larger 4-wheel trolley was common by *circa* 1900. They soon became slightly shorter and gained a raised lip around the trolley platform to enable safe loading with churns to the full width of the vehicle. For ordinary parcels and cases, this feature must have reduced losses and damage too. Initially, they were equipped with large cast iron wheels, later replaced with smaller cast iron wheels with or without solid rubber tyres. These duly became the norm and platform luggage scales were designed especially for their use. Parcels traffic was charged by weight, so barrows all carried an inscription or plate stating their tare weight. At larger stations, where electric tugs were used, such trolleys were fitted with couplings front and rear. Many will recall those long trains of barrows, skilfully being driven through the crowds at Paddington. The views of these 4-wheel trolleys were taken at Totnes.

Rule 21a (GWR Rule Book 1933).

"Luggage and parcels must not, where the width of the platform will admit, be left within six feet of the edge of the platform; platform trollies, barrows etc., not in use must be kept back close to the buildings or to the wall or fence at the back of the platform, with their handles so placed as to avoid the risk of persons stumbling over the, When necessary, platform trollies, barrows etc., must be so secured as to prevent them from moving."

21b. "Unauthorised persons must not be allowed to use trollies, barrows etc."

Above: Two wheelers were commonplace in the Edwardian era, proving more stable than the single wheel version and so capable of carrying a greater load. They were more manoeuvrable than the 4-wheeled type although consideration of the porter's comfort was then less of an issue. Into the mid-1960s, busy resort stations like Torquay hired temporary porter staff in high season. They were known as 'Out station porters' who for a small fee and hoped-for tip would wheel luggage from station to boarding house or hotel. This useful income for an impecunious student could be hard-earned.

Initially, these two wheelers appear to have had a single hoop upon which to stack the luggage. Later, additional cross bracing was added together with a 'mudguard'. The cast iron wheels were noisy and in later years were often replaced with solid rubber tyres. On crowded platforms, there was a risk of catching people's ankles, and perhaps as a result of such an incident, the outside-framed version came about. At first they appear to have been unique to Paddington but odd ones were noted further afield in later years. The outside frame version is clearly a simple adaptation of the norm. This pair is at Didcot, where there is also an example of the Paddington type, bearing what looks like an ancient coat of Royal Mail red paint – perhaps a 'one-off'. These were largely displaced by the BRUTE trolley.

Upper views: For dealing with crates and heavier consignments, Goods Dept sack trucks like this were used from the early 1900s. Note the V notch in the plate to facilitate tying a cord around the load. It would seem that this type of steel support leg was not up to the job and by the 1930s had been mainly replaced by a heavy wooden block. This unaltered survivor has found a home at Staverton on the South Devon Railway.

Right: At sheds and repair depots, heavy toolboxes and large lumps of engine demanded something particularly robust. This type was short and more stoutly constructed typically with different wheels. The curved iron plate formed a well on the back of the lower part of the handles. Also seen at Staverton but historically it would not have appeared at such a rural location.

Bottom left: This lightweight design is rarer and appears to have been used at Goods depots. This example is in the steam railway museum at Launceston. It does not seem to have ever been painted, except for the lettering.

Opposite bottom and bottom right: A couple of examples of lettering which shew that colours were not always standardised.

Editorial Comment: Readers may note that most illustrations for this article are drawn from the preservation scene in apparent contravention of the policy detailed in the Introduction on Page 3. The article was accepted for publication before all details of editorial policy had been agreed; its welcome inclusion helps demonstrate how much interest can derive from even quite mundane subjects associated with the Old Company.

READING SIGNAL WORKS

Unlike Swindon, the Signalling Department at Reading has received little attention in published form, and information about its history and activities is scarce. Even the *Great Western Magazine* had little to say on the subject, preferring to accord precedence to locomotive, rolling stock, stations and routes. Signalling and everything that went with it was largely by-passed in railway literature. Many photographic records are incidental to the traditional three-quarter view of locomotive and train with signals off to one side. This is a pity as the works located to the north side of Reading station, and before that the Telegraph Department at Paddington, were responsible for the vast array of equipment within each signal box and at the lineside that was essential for the safe and efficient running of the railway. Reading was also headquarters for the network of subsidiary departments throughout the system. These were mainly located at the principal station within the company's divisional structure; those units maintained their own stores facilities and undertook routine maintenance.

In the earliest years, equipment was purchased from commercial manufacturers e.g. the initial telegraph installed between Paddington and Slough was supplied by Messrs Cooke and Wheatstone. Expansion of the national network saw establishment of numerous independent manufacturers and contractors to produce and install equipment developed by this burgeoning technology. Resultant names became synonymous with signalling hardware (The Railway Signalling Co., Evans O'Donnell, McKenzie & Holland, Westinghouse etc) while others specialised in provision of interior equipment (Sykes, Spagnoletti etc).

In the early days, the Signal Department was controlled by the GWR's Chief Engineer (and later the Engineer's Department) with responsibility for provision and maintenance of all signals and locking gear. The actual position of Chief Engineer lapsed with the retirement of W G Owen in 1885 (**1**).

The GWR's incursion into manufacture of its own signalling equipment dates from establishment of the Reading workshops in 1855 under Thomas Blackall (**2**). This initiative formed part of the company's drive towards self-sufficiency. This objective also embraced manufacture of cranes, girders, footbridges, permanent-way fittings and

Opposite: This was the pedestrian entrance to Reading Signal Works, looking out towards Caversham Road with part of the modern fire station just visible in the right background. The structure of the gate house suggests that this could have been one of the original works buildings. Security guard on duty

This page: Looking south along Caversham Road with the main line crossing by the distant bridge. The large brick building formed part of the signal works. The main entrance is just discernible beside the distant pedestrian on the left. The is an official GWR photograph dated June 1937 when trams were still operating along Caversham Road; these services ceased in May 1939. Following demolition of the works, the site passed into non-railway use and ironically a road sign appeared on the footpath 'New Signals Ahead' (referring to road traffic and sadly not the railway).

associated equipment, plus most of the Engineering Department's wagons. The casting of individual components was always carried out at Swindon, and supplied to Reading as required

The first locking frame was produced by Reading works in 1863, to the design of Michael Lane (according to one source) who was Chief Engineer from 1860 to 1868. However, MacDermot acknowledges Blackall in this regard although it was customary for a department's most senior officer to be credited with all work undertaken by subordinates. A century and a half later, true credit is impossible to confirm and while a Patent was probably sought, the National Archives advise *'The nineteenth and early twentieth century registers and indexes of patents and trademarks formerly in BT 73, BT 74, BT 75 (patents) and BT 80, BT 81, BT 86, and BT 92 (trade marks) were destroyed in 1963 in accordance with the Public Records Act 1958, with the exception of a few specimens transferred to BT*

900.' *https://discovery.nationalarchives.gov.uk/ details/r/C479* .

MacDermot (page 497) says that Blackall also designed signals (of the disc and crossbar type produced until November 1869) and that while some locking frames and signals were erected by contractors, mainly Messrs Saxby & Farmer, the majority were built by the GWR.

Blackall's responsibilities at Reading expanded to take in all new work (whether this was confined to signalling matters or included other equipment is unclear) but by then routine maintenance was conducted by Divisional Engineers. As an example, the late Larry Crosier possessed a notebook relative to the Exeter Division in which the local engineer had drawn the positioning of all signals required on new lines such as the Exe Valley route. The necessary equipment would have been ordered from Reading.

This is a post-war view of the signal works yard with the end wall of an air raid shelter in the centre. Timber or concrete lengths have been stacked alongside and also on the roof. A pannier tank is lurking on the siding in the left background. This yard was used for storage of larger items including signal posts, level crossing gates, concrete troughs and point rodding. (In the 1980s some concrete signal posts that probably dated from around World War 1 were still lying among some brambles). The 1922 track diagrams (similar to those for the Henley-on-Thames branch appearing later in this issue), indicate that a small engine shed was also provided. No images have been located but it would have stood behind the photographer. Rail access was through the adjacent coal yard and also *via* several reverse moves into what was known as No 6 road on the north side of the station.

Blackall retired from what was an expanding department early in 1893 and the Signalling Department was then placed in the charge of William Dean. This was ostensibly a strange choice but possibly related to the castings situation mentioned earlier. Nevertheless, Reading continued as the centre for signal design and development and Alfred Thomas Blackall (born 1858 and son of Thomas) was appointed as an 'Assistant' until succeeding as Engineer in charge of the newly independent Signal Department in August 1897. The final expansion occurred in 1903 with absorption of the former Telegraph Department, previously been based at Paddington.

It should be noted that the Great Western Study Group has published *GWR Signalling Practice*, certainly the most comprehensive history to date, and wholeheartedly recommended. However,

Reading is limited and we would welcome readers' additional information (and photographs) on the works and its products. Aside from the Signalling Record Society, reference is also made to www.signalworks.co.uk where an extensive list of known drawings produced at Reading can be found. This also includes numerous non-signal related items and which evidently goes back to the earliest days.

[1] MacDermot is confusing on Owen's departure, referring to it both as a resignation and then elsewhere as retirement. On the basis of age and previous work undertaken including being involved with the abolition of the broad gauge in places, he probably retired.

[2] The surname Blackall appears synonymous with the GWR for several generations. For example, one Thomas Blackall was the regular driver of No 111 *The Great Bear*, while there were at least two members of the Blackall family employed as signalmen at Reading in the latter days of mechanical signalling.

The core activity of the signal works was the manufacture of lever frames which would be erected on-site for assembly and testing of the locking mechanisms. These would then be dismantled for shipment to the intended location. The frame in this undated view appears to comprise 89 levers, excluding spaces. Two men are engaged in testing the mechanisms and at this stage the levers would be easy to move being only connected to the locking mechanism. They are working about 12 feet above the ground level with little concession to safety.

Above: Two double-deck Spagnoletti block instruments are visible on the desk in the "Telegraph test shop", a title retained long after this activity had been amalgamated with the Signalling Department. The company used a wide range of Tablet, Token and Staff instruments. Other interior signal box equipment was generally made at Reading although recourse was necessary to commercial manufacturers during times of high demand - war time expansion for example.

Track layouts varied widely and some were unique to specific signal boxes, particularly at junctions, yards and larger stations. It was therefore sometimes more economic to purchase from specialist manufacturers. Company-produced items were largely standardised but among bespoke instruments supplied by outside firms, some examples were quite rare.

Early in the 20th Century, the company produced a catalogue of "Signal Fittings" for different forms of outside equipment, (signal arms, pulleys, cranks etc). Apparently, this was never re-issued in full but was up-dated to take account of new equipment as when metal posts replaced the traditional timber type. The incomplete nature of this information raises questions where readers might be able to assist:

- Was there ever an indoor equipment version of the Signal Fittings catalogue?

- Regarding lever frames, the traditional brass lever leads (i.e. the brass plate on which was engraved the lever number and the leads that had to be pulled to enable its release) were replaced by ivorine plates. It is believed that this occurred before World War 2 but can specific date(s) be verified?

- Under GWR practice, lever frames with the block shelf above faced the running lines, a logical layout that worked well. This was apparently changed in BR days to follow LMS and SR practice whereby the lever frame faced the rear wall. Does anyone know when this change was instituted?

Opposite top: 0-6-0ST Class 850 No. 1925 saw out its career as the works shunter. Built at Wolverhampton in 1883, it had been a Reading resident for some years and had earlier worked regularly on the Lambourn branch. The small panniers were handy engines, and sufficiently highly regarded for BR Western Region to build seventy of Class 16xx as a modern version of Class 2021, which had followed Class 850. No 1925 was a celebrity as it never acquired pannier tanks and survived as the last 0-6-0ST, excluding the youngsters of Class 1361 that dated from 1910.

Opposite bottom: There was a time when a lineman or a gang from the S&T department would travel to a work site by train. Their equipment would either accompany them on a special train, or would be sent ahead by a local goods working. Modernisation eventually arrived *circa* 1957 with vehicles such as this Karrier 'Gamecock' with a bespoke body to carry 11 men and equipment.

Reading was also the centre for repair of the company's time pieces including station clocks, brass signal box drum clocks, and guard's watches. In later years some former station clocks found their way into signal boxes to replace the original drum type. The view opposite shows part of the clock repair facility within the main works. The view above, dated 20 May 1948 shows clock repairs being undertaken in the former Reading Middle Signal Box which had been decommissioned in 1896. This room seems also to be in use for cabinet repairs judging by the sawdust which would hardly seem compatible with clockwork mechanisms. (One of the editors recalls visiting the stores at Swindon in the late 1980s and seeing a room almost full of GWR long case clocks which had been literally thrown on top of each other.)

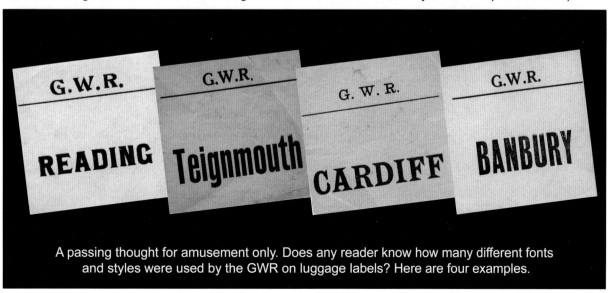

A passing thought for amusement only. Does any reader know how many different fonts and styles were used by the GWR on luggage labels? Here are four examples.

THE STATION DIAGRAM BOOKS

As part of its operating procedures, the GWR produced a series of books based on the respective divisions that provided a schematic reference to each station, junction, goods yard and depot. Additional information included the lengths of platforms and loops, and the capacity of each siding measured in 4-wheel wagon lengths. The editorial team holds a copy of the Diagram Book for the London Division and others exist in the National Archives. However, if a reader has a copy for other divisions, we would be grateful for a short term loan for copying and future reference purposes.

Without being able to effect comparisons, precise dating is difficult but that for the London division is *circa* 1920. The whole system was possibly mapped around that time, and we are not aware of any subsequent updates. Larger locations like Paddington, Reading and Oxford took up several folded sides preventing reproduction to a readable

scale. Consequently, the samples here have been selected as they fit the page size.

These diagrams were important for the department of the Superintendent of the Line although experienced clerks were doubtless familiar with the details of regularly used locations. As an example, the Shiplake diagram advises that the maximum capacity of the two sidings is 28 wagons. Hence a freight train bound for that destination could not exceed that number, or possibly less if the sidings were already partially occupied. Allowance also had to be made for engine and brake van if the train was to be shunted clear of the main line. Further, the island platform length (in this case 600 feet) was important in planning the working of special passenger services that might use this station.

As the principal carrier of both goods and passengers, the railways would invariably have

Above: Looking south along the 500' platforms at Wargrave towards Henley-on-Thames.

Opposite: Page 83 from the Station Diagrams Book features the Henley-on-Thames branch, with distances measured from the main line junction at Twyford. In this case, siding capacities were defined in 20-foot wagon lengths 'but exclusive of any engine or (brake) van'. There must have been a process to convert this dimension to an equivalent in passenger stock, particularly to cope with stabling of special trains during Regatta week.

The position of the signal boxes is shown but without any technical details. Also, the footbridge between the platforms at Wargrave has been omitted.

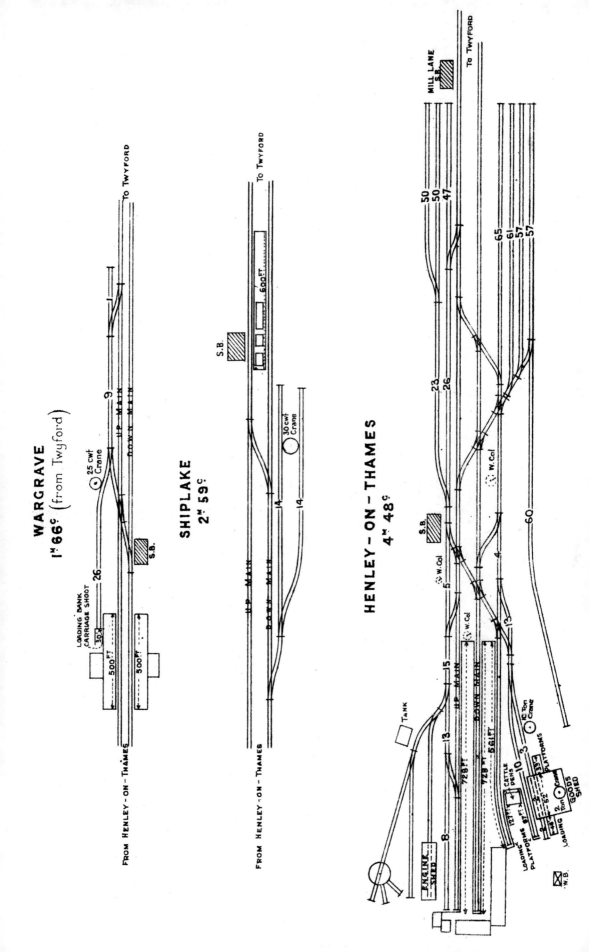

WARGRAVE
1ᴹ 66ᶜ (from Twyford)

25 cwt Crane

LOADING BANK
CARRIAGE SHOOT

30 FT

500 FT

500 FT

S.B.

26

9

UP MAIN

DOWN MAIN

To TWYFORD

FROM HENLEY-ON-THAMES

SHIPLAKE
2ᴹ 59ᶜ

S.B.

600 FT

30 cwt Crane

14

14

UP MAIN

DOWN MAIN

To TWYFORD

FROM HENLEY-ON-THAMES

HENLEY-ON-THAMES
4ᴹ 48ᶜ

MILL LANE S.B.

To TWYFORD

50

50

47

65

61

57

57

23

26

S.B.

W.Col

W.Col

60

4

13

5

15

13

TANK

ENGINE SHED

UP MAIN

DOWN MAIN

728 FT

728 FT

561 FT

W.Col

10 Ton Crane

CATTLE PENS

LOADING PLATFORMS

GOODS SHED

2 Ton Crane

PLATFORMS

8

13

52

33

10

3

2

2

W.B.

stock stabled in the various sidings. Unless siding rental agreements were in place, private owner (usually coal) wagons were time-restricted for unloading purposes before demurrage was incurred. The system was far from perfect and it was not unusual for wagons to be temporarily 'lost'. It was usual for station masters to be instructed to check sidings for vehicles and to report their running numbers. This was especially important when a loaded wagon had been incorrectly marshalled leading to delivery to an incorrect destination, and thus to complaints from the consignor/ consignee.

At one quiet rural station, we were told that the station master was a regular recipient of instructions to check for the missing wagons. Despite being able to view the full length of his empire (two sidings) from his office, an instruction from Paddington was sacrosanct. He would therefore walk the length of his usually empty yard so that he could honestly write 'yard checked, vehicles not present' and return the enquiry with a clear conscience.

Above: Shiplake looking south towards the junction at Twyford. The footbridge which was the photographer's vantage point was omitted from the diagram despite providing access to the island platform. Ground level pedestrian access was also possible from the level crossing (also omitted) that dissected the station i.e. the sidings were on the north side. At one time camping coaches were provided both here and at Wargrave.

Opposite: General view of Henley-on-Thames showing the canopy extension installed in 1904. Although the diagram defined the platform lengths and siding capacities, no information was provided on the turntable diameter or those sidings that were solely used by the locomotive department. This reflects different divisional responsibilities 'on the ground' as provision of motive power was not the province of the Traffic department. Doubtless the locomotive department was well aware of the maximum permissible engine size. Henley was known to host Stars and Halls engaged on working Regatta Week specials.

Opposite: Two further views taken at Salisbury but again the dates are unknown. However, "Flying Banana" No 11 officially entered traffic on 17th February 1936 and it is clearly in new condition. There were varying seating layouts in railcars No 1 to 16 and this example had accommodation for 63 passengers plus a single toilet. Although reasonably powerful with two engines and gearboxes, the lack of drawgear prevented the haulage of a trailer coach. It is believed that the pattern of traffic over the Bristol-Westbury-Salisbury section never favoured the regular use of single railcars so this was probably a test working. It has certainly excited the interest of the other company's personnel to the right as the Southern had nothing like it. The streamlined modernity must have been a thought-provoking vision of what the future might hold. No 11 was first allocated to Weymouth. It was still there in January 1938 but had moved to Oxford by 31st December 1947. By 1950, it was allocated to Landore, from where it was withdrawn in November 1957.

From *The Railway Gazette*,

13 March 1914.

"A curious incident, fortunately unattended by any serious results, happened on the Great Western Railway near Twyford station on 6 March.

"There is a water trough some miles to the west of Reading station and water was picked up from this trough by the water scoop fitted to the tender of an express passenger train from Plymouth. The scoop appears to have been perfectly safe to travel, but on account of the fastenings not being made secure there was nothing to retain it in the raised position, and it gradually worked down until it was riding slight below rail level. It proceeded without coming into contact with any portion of the permanent way until the engine was passing over a ramp fixed in the middle of the 4 ft way about a quarter of a mile west of Twyford station. The ramp consisted three sections of inverted 'T' iron, measuring in all 60 ft., and is used in connection with the Great Western pattern of automatic train control. As the ramp is slightly higher than rail level and the scoop was riding improperly in the lowered position, the scoop came into contact with the ramp, and after stripping all three portions of the 'T' iron from their mountings, caused one of the pieces to lodge in the woodwork of the leading coach and to protrude through the roof, as shown in the accompanying illustration. The train was promptly stopped and afterwards proceeded safely to its destination. It is fortunate that the scoop came in contact with a comparatively unresisting obstacle and that nothing more serious happened."

MODERNISING THE WESTERN: PART 1 - LAIRA

Great Western Railway, British Railways Western Region, and then British Rail Western Region were corporate identities carried by the system in the last 30 years of this publication's survey period, well before the complexity of privatisation, sectorisation, and train operating companies changed so much of the national network's public face and organisational structures.

Modernisation on a comprehensive scale really commenced with the largely ill-fated 1955 nationwide scheme. The incursion of BR Mark 1 coaching stock and livery changes had been earlier signs of contemporary trends which were soon followed by steam locomotive replacement. Early infrastructural improvements initially focussed on meeting the maintenance needs of the new technology, just as in 1906 John Armstrong had overseen the creation of Old Oak Common to cope with the locomotives required to handle more, faster and heavier trains.

Half a century later, another construction programme was in hand at Plymouth Laira to cope with the fresh demands that would be presented by the next motive power generation. Although distant from London, this location had particular advantages. There was plenty of room available for a greenfield site development that would be physically isolated from the dirty environment of the old depot. It helped satisfy the early priority for steam replacement in the far west to ease the expense of moving substantial tonnages of locomotive coal from South Wales. This had been a recurrent issue and one reason for the GWR's investigation of electrification west of Taunton on at least two occasions in the inter-war period. On completion, Laira Diesel was one of the first modern maintenance facilities on British Railways. It continues in this role today, having witnessed key changes in the nature of diesel power.

Above: Almost considered heretical at the time, Dick Riley recorded aspects of the new Laira facility then under construction during his West Country jaunts between 1960 and 1962. Dated 17 July 1960, the first view shows progress on what was the first of three buildings served by four roads on the west side of the site. Originally intended for servicing and maintenance, No. 1 road was equipped with a wheel lathe and lifting jacks for bogie exchange. There are sundry wagons loaded with building supplies standing on the approach roads. To the extreme right in the distance can just be seen some diesel locomotives stabled outside the old shed. Laira steam depot officially closed on 13 June 1965.

Opposite: Two months later Dick recorded construction from a slightly different angle. Central to this view is the Heavy Maintenance Shed whose height allowed engine units to be lifted clear and replaced on what became roads 5 and 6. The entire complex was built from reinforced concrete and with many windows to render a light and airy interior. The steam shed's coal stage of the steam shed is visible to the right across an inlet known as Cattlewater which feeds into the River Plym. NBL Class 63xx Type 2 diesel-hydraulics are stabled together with a 'Castle'. There are also some depot breakdown train vans and an ex-auto coach in departmental service. *To be continued in Issue 2.*

THE GUARD'S COMPARTMENT

Western Times welcomes constructive comment from readers either by way of additional information on subjects already published, or suggestions for new topics to be addressed. The diversity of departments outlined above illustrates the breadth and complexity of a large company that in many respects was self-sufficient. The editors see it as their remit over time to explore all these nooks and crannies.

Issue No 2 will continue the theme of variety with more about divisional responsibilities, locomotive types, and West Country dieselisation. The railway in wartime, panniers in Scotland, Colwell tunnel and the Safety Movement will also be under the spotlight. We reiterate that contributions from readers will be welcome and fees will be paid for published articles.

Please step aboard this train back to the great days of the GWR and BR(WR)!

WesternTimes@mail.com